MEN-AT-A
THE US AF

Text by
PHILIP KATCHER
Colour plates by
CHRIS COLLINGWOOD

Published in 1985 by
Osprey Publishing Ltd
59 Grosvenor Street, London W1X 9DA
© Copyright 1984 Osprey Publishing Ltd
Reprinted 1985, 1986, 1987, 1988, 1989, 1990, 1991

British Library Cataloguing in Publication Data
Katcher, Philip
    The US Army, 1941–45. —(Men-at-Arms
    series; 70)
    1. United States.   *Army*—Uniforms—History
    I. Title   II. Series
    355.1'4'0973   UC483

    ISBN 0-85045-522-7

Filmset in Great Britain
Printed in Hong Kong

Introduction

In the original edition of this title, published in 1977, the author attempted to give a summary of various aspects of uniform practice, particular insignia, organisation, combat deployment of divisions, and so on. In this revised edition, in response to the expressed interests of the growing number of uniform collectors on both sides of the Atlantic, the scope of the text has been limited to a detailed examination of uniform items, drawing upon official sources. The colour plates have been prepared from these official contemporary sources, confirmed by wartime photographs and by examination of surviving examples of all the items illustrated.

*   *   *

The United States Army took an unusual approach, for the period, towards the design of its uniforms. Rather than attempt to find an all-purpose uniform, such as the British battledress, it attempted to design special-purpose dress for every possible duty, from combat in cold climates to dress parades in hot ones.

According to the 1942 edition of *The Officers' Guide*: 'There are many kinds of uniforms, each for a definite purpose, which are required or authorised to be worn. Few officers own all of them. The wool service uniform may be said to be the only one required to be in the possession of all officers of the Army of the United States. The cotton service uniform is prescribed for summer wear at nearly all stations, although officers are privileged to wear the woollen uniform, if they wish to do so, while the troops are in cotton. It is customary, however, for officers on duty with troop units to wear the type which is prescribed for troops.'

The specific types of uniforms listed are the wool service uniform with coat, the wool service uniform

The khaki shirt and trousers worn as combat dress, 1941. (US Army)

with olive-drab shirt, the service cotton uniform with cotton or wool olive-drab shirt, and the fatigue uniform of olive-drab herringbone twill. Dress uniforms included the full dress uniform, the blue dress uniform, the full dress or blue dress uniform for mounted officers, the blue mess uniform, the white dress uniform, and the white mess uniform. Special uniforms were authorised for flying, armoured forces, parachute units, aviation cadets, ski troops and arctic service.

The basic field uniform for officers included a garrison or 'overseas' cap, service shirt and trousers, a field jacket when weather required it, Army russet brown leather high shoes, canvas gaiters or high russet brown boots, identification tags, a weapon and web field equipment. The same uniform served for field service for enlisted men. Some substitutions could be made, such as a long or short overcoat for officers, or a long overcoat for enlisted men, instead of the field jacket. Additions could also be made, such as the sweater designed for wear under the M1941 field jacket.

A variation of this dress was called the 'work

uniform', and it included a herringbone twill cap or hat, gloves when necessary, service shoes, and a one-piece or two-piece herringbone twill suit or shirt and trousers, with identification tags. The one-piece suit was to be worn by members of the armoured forces and mechanics, while everyone else was to wear the two-piece suit. Weapons and field equipment would also be carried.

Civilians serving with the armed forces in the field were to wear the appropriate officer's uniform, without rank insignia but with the regulation brassard. There were a number of such civilians with the Army, ranging from postal employees to newspaper correspondents.

All uniforms were, according to Field Manual 21–15, to be kept clean and neat and in good repair. Missing insignia and buttons were to be quickly replaced. Overcoats, coats and shirts were always to be buttoned. The emphasis, however, especially in the field, was more on comfort and ease of use of uniform, equipment and weapons than strictly on appearance. This has been the emphasis in the uniform and equipment philosophy of the United States Army throughout its history.

The final result was that US troops in the field, especially in Europe, did not always appear to have the 'soldierly' qualities often displayed by both the enemy and the other Allies. On 5 May 1943 Capt. Harry C. Butcher, USN, public relations aide to Gen. Dwight D. Eisenhower, noted in his diary: 'Ike

US Army combat uniforms of 1941, posed in front of the US Capitol Building; the men are as embarassed as soldiers always are when forced to play-act, but the uniforms are interesting. Left to right: a soldier equipped for snow-shoe operations; the summer khaki dismounted uniform; the winter dismounted uniform; the winter armoured trooper's uniform; the ski operation uniform; a paratrooper, fitted out for this shot in an Air Corps seat-type parachute; and the summer mounted uniform. (US Army)

has been impressed by the virtual impossibility of American officers and soldiers appearing neat and snappy in their field uniforms. He has suggested to Gen. [George C.] Marshall [Army Chief of Staff] that the Quartermaster begin now to have designed another winter uniform for next winter's wear. He thought the material should be rough wool because it wouldn't show the dirt and is more easily kept presentable. He liked the appearance of the British battledress, but thought Americans should design something distinctive for themselves. He thought our head covering was not too good—the helmet is splendid, and its stocking cap inter-lining is suitable for wear outside the combat zone. While on pass, or working at rear headquarters, the overseas cap is acceptable. He thinks that sloppy fatigue hats and mechanics' caps should be abolished, as most GIs [slang for an enlisted man, from *Government Issue*] seem to prefer them to more soldierly headgear. He has issued an order prohibiting the wearing of fatigue hats in North Africa.'

Gen. George S. Patton went further, fining soldiers in his command for wearing the knit M1941 wool cap without wearing a helmet over it. Even so, it turned out to be impossible to keep the American volunteer soldier looking anything like a 'picture book' soldier, and, in the end, comfort prevailed over appearance.

Uniform Colours

According to the 1942 8th Edition of *The Officers' Guide*: 'Prescribed articles of service uniforms or outer clothing, except such articles specified as of "commercial pattern", will conform in quality, design, and color to the corresponding approved samples and published specifications.'

Unfortunately, the Army Regulations governing uniforms blandly throw around the term 'olive-drab' for virtually everything, when in fact vastly different shades of olive-drab were called for. It was not until the 31 March 1944 AR 600–35 was published that specific shades were described, and then only by number.

It was impossible to be too pedantic about the exact shade of everything. *The Officers' Guide* recognised this when making suggestions on what

The winter field uniform included a garrison (overseas) cap with arm-of-service coloured piping, the M1941 field jacket, wool trousers, gaiters and service shoes. (US Army)

An officer's coat, to 1944 regulation standard. These were privately made, and details of lining and labels vary. The only label in this example bears the US coat of arms and 'REGULATION ARMY OFFICER'S COAT.' The insignia is that of a Signal Corps officer, with an American Campaign medal ribbon and an expert rifleman's badge. (All close-ups of uniform items are from the author's collection unless otherwise indicated.)

purchased, it is desirable to select the drab or lighter shade. For arduous service, the trousers issued by the Quartermaster to enlisted men and sold to officers are entirely satisfactory. However, because of variation in shade, it would be bizarre to wear these trousers with a standard officer's service coat.'

According to AR 600–35, 31 March 1944, the official shades were: for service and garrison caps, olive-drab shade No.51 (dark shade); for breeches and trousers, either olive-drab shade No.51 (dark shade) or drab shade No.54 (light shade); for wool shirts, either olive-drab shade No.51 (dark shade), drab shade No.54 (light shade), khaki shade No.1, or olive-drab shade No.50; for cotton shirts, khaki shade No.1, and for short officers' overcoats, olive-drab shade No.52. For long officers' overcoats the colour was olive-drab shades No.2 and No.7. The M1943 field jacket was to be olive-drab shade No.7. Every piece of the summer uniform, including coats, breeches, trousers, shirts, and garrison and service caps, was to be khaki shade No.1. Neckties were to be khaki shade No.5.

Special cards were produced by a private association in New York showing exactly what these shades were to be, and including dye information, for manufacturers. These cards can still be obtained through the modern counterpart of that organisation, now called The Color Association of the United States, 24 East 38th Street, New York NY 10016, USA.

wool trousers a new officer should buy:

'A good chance to make an unwise purchase is presented in the choice of wool trousers as to color. Olive-drab (dark shade) trousers are prescribed for wear by officers when in the field. Drab (light shade) trousers may be worn by officers at other times. Drab trousers are an article optional with the individual officer (Par. 35, AR 600–40).

'The light-colored trousers are advantageous in one important respect in that they can be worn with any service coat. Due to fading and variation in dyes, the olive-drab dark shade trousers are worn properly only with the service coat made from the same cloth. Tables of Basic Allowances prescribe that the officer must provide two pairs of trousers, and that is certainly a minimum to allow for dry cleaning. In satisfaction of this requirement, olive-drab (dark shade) is advised. If a third pair is

Uniform Regulations

Uniforms according to AR 600–35, 10 November 1941

Officers' and Warrant Officers' service coat
General description from Army Regulation 600–35: 'A single-breasted collar and lapel coat; lining, if desired to be same color as coat. To fit easy over the chest and shoulders and to be fitted slightly at the waist to conform to the figure so as to prevent wrinkling or rolling under the leather belt when worn. The back to have two side plaits[1] not less than 3 inches in depth at shoulders and to extend from shoulder seam where it joins the armhole seam to waistline, buttoned down the front with four large

[1] In British parlance, 'pleats'.

regulation coat buttons equally spaced. The crossing of the lapels will be approximately $1\frac{3}{4}$ inches above the top button.

'To support the belt, except for officers of the Army Air Forces, two metal hooks of the same material as the metal trimmings on the leather belt will be let into the side seams at the waistline.

'For officers of the Army Air Forces, the coat will have a belt approximately 2 inches wide of the same material as the coat, sewed down all around the waistline, with the bottom button placed slightly below the sewed-on belt.

'There will be four outside pockets, two upper and two lower, covered with flaps, buttoned with small regulation coat buttons at the center and placed so that the upper lines are horizontal. The two upper pockets to be patch pockets, slightly rounded at the lower corners, with a box plait $1\frac{1}{2}$ inches in width on the vertical center line. The flaps to be rounded slightly at the corners and reaching to a slight point at the center. The flap buttons to be in line with the top buttons of the coat.

'The two lower pockets to be hung inside the body of the skirt, covered by flaps with the lower corners slightly rounded and the lower edge horizontal. The pockets to be attached to the body of the skirt only at the mouth. The top lines of the lower pocket flaps to be placed slightly below the waistline.

'On each shoulder a loop of the same material as the coat, let in at the sleeve head seam and reaching to approximately $\frac{3}{4}$ inch beneath the collar,

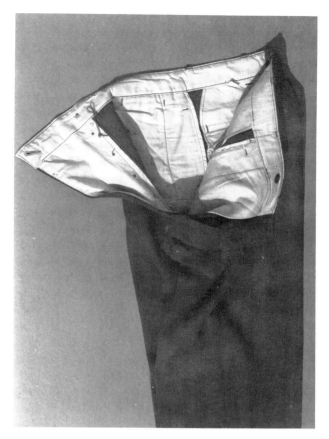

The olive drab wool issue enlisted man's trousers; there are two rear hip pockets, two slash side pockets and a watch pocket at the front of the right hip. There is a button fly; all pockets and inside linings are of white cotton duck. Underneath the right side pocket is a white label printed in black 'TROUSERS, WOOL, SERGE, O.D./SPECIAL LIGHT SHADE/ Stock 4557–86632/ 30 × 31/M. FINE & SONS/MFG. CO. INC./ P.O. No.3391/ Dated Oct.17,1941/Spec. P.Q.D. No. 353/Dated April 17, 1943/ Phila. Q.M. Depot'.

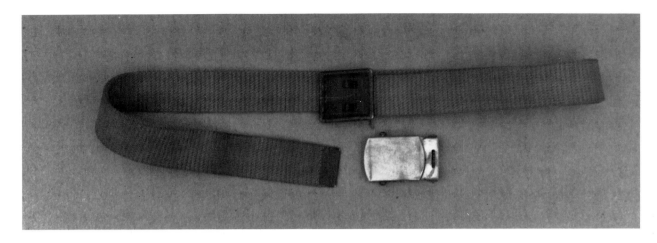

The khaki web issue belt, marked 'U.S.' inside near the buckle and dated 1943. The black frame buckle is the issue enlisted man's type; the brass plate buckle was to be worn by officers only.

buttoning at the collar edge with a small regulation coat button. Loops to be about $2\frac{1}{2}$ inches in width at the lower end and $1\frac{1}{2}$ inches in width at the collar edge and cross-stitched down to shoulder for a distance from about 2 inches from lower end.

'The skirt to be full with a slight flare, and to extend 1 to 2 inches below the crotch, according to the height of the wearer, with a slit in the back extending from the waistline to the bottom of the skirt following the back seam with an underlap of approximately $2\frac{1}{2}$ inches. The front overlapping left edge of coat to be cut with a pronounced flare to the right from the bottom button to the bottom of the skirt, so as to appear straight from the lapel opening to the bottom of the coat and to remain overlapped not less than 4 inches when in a standing position, without the use of hooks and eyes, the fullness necessary to accomplish this result being over the hips.

'For officers a band of olive-drab braid $\frac{1}{2}$ inch in width on each sleeve, the lower edge 3 inches from end of sleeve. For warrant officers and enlisted men who served honorably as commissioned officers in the World War a similar band of forest green braid similarly placed. Other warrant officers will have no braid on the sleeves.'

Officers' overcoat
'A double-breasted ulster with convertible style roll collar and notch lapel, lining of same color as ulster; buttoned down the front with a double row of large regulation overcoat buttons, three on each side

below the roll of the lapel with the top buttons approximately $6\frac{1}{2}$ to 7 inches apart; a button placed under the right collar and a buttonhole at the top of each lapel, one for use when collar is converted and the other for appearance; the lining slit and fastened to pocket openings to allow the hand to go through to pocket of breeches or trousers; slit closed with a small button and buttonhole. Back to be plaited and to have back straps let into the side seam at the waistline, fastened together with two large regulation buttons and buttonholes. Skirt not longer than 10 inches or shorter than 3 inches below the knee; slit in the back extending from bottom of back strap to bottom of skirt and closing with small concealed buttons and buttonholes. The front corners to be provided with buttons and buttonholes so that the corners may be turned back to facilitate marching.

'Two outside welted pockets, one on each side, with vertical openings; the center of pocket about opposite lower button and placed on a line with front seam of sleeve.

'On each shoulder a loop about 5 inches in length, $2\frac{1}{2}$ inches in width at the lower end and $1\frac{1}{2}$ inches in width at the upper end, which is slightly pointed, same material as the coat, let in at the sleeve head seam, buttoning at the upper end with a small regulation overcoat button.'

Officers were to have plain sleeves, except for generals, who were to wear 'two bands of black braid, the lower band to be $1\frac{1}{4}$ inches in width and about $2\frac{1}{2}$ inches from the lower edge of the sleeve, the other to be $\frac{1}{2}$ inch in width and $1\frac{1}{2}$ inches above the lower band.'

Officers' short overcoat
'A double-breasted coat, lined or unlined, with a

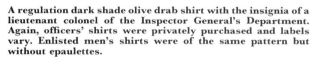

A regulation dark shade olive drab shirt with the insignia of a lieutenant colonel of the Inspector General's Department. Again, officers' shirts were privately purchased and labels vary. Enlisted men's shirts were of the same pattern but without epaulettes.

The M1941 field jacket, lined with thin blanket wool. The '36 L' label indicates size in inches round the chest, and 'long'; 'R' and 'S' stood for 'regular' and 'small'. There are no other labels in this jacket, which bears the left shoulder patch of the 101st Airborne Division, and lieutenant colonel's rank leaves on the epaulettes.

shawl roll collar approximately 5 inches in width, buttoned down the front with a double row of large regulation overcoat buttons, three on each side below the roll of collar with additional buttons or loops so that the coat can be buttoned to the neck. A detachable belt of the same material as coat, held in place with loops sewed on at side seams.

'Two outside patch pockets, one on each side.

'On each shoulder a loop about 5 inches in length, $2\frac{1}{2}$ inches in width at lower end and $1\frac{1}{2}$ inches in width at the upper end, which is slightly pointed, of same material as coat, let in at the sleeve head seam and buttoned at the upper end with small regulation overcoat button.

'Skirt to extend to 6 inches above the knee. Slit in the back extending about 15 inches from the bottom.'

Cuff decoration was the same as for the long overcoats.

Officers' and Warrant Officers' raincoat
'A waterproof coat of commercial pattern, with shoulder loops, as nearly as practicable olive-drab color.'

Officers' and enlisted men's dress gloves
'Chamois leather or chamois color material', or 'white cotton or lisle.'

Officers' and enlisted men's service gloves
'Leather of light russet color, lined or unlined, snap fastener, pull-on or buckle type', or 'wool, olive-drab.'

Officers' service cap
'Of adopted design about $11\frac{1}{4}$ inches from front to rear and $10\frac{1}{2}$ inches from side to side, based on size $7\frac{1}{8}$, stiffened in front by springs and falling without stiffening to the rear; two eyelets $\frac{1}{2}$ inch from the welt seam and about $\frac{3}{4}$ inch on each side of side seam of quarters. Top to be stiffened at rim with grommet and cloth on top of crown to be slack. The grommet

used to stiffen the rim will be flat $\frac{3}{16}$ inch in width (measurements of crown above to be made with grommet in position in cap), inside of top to have a waterproof material cut to the size of the crown.

'Top of visor of Army russet leather lined with embossed green hatters' leather, waterproofed. Greatest width of visor about $2\frac{3}{16}$ inches and slope from vertical about 55 degrees.

'Chinstrap of Army russet leather $\frac{3}{4}$ inch in width and $9\frac{1}{2}$ inches in length fastened at each end of visor with small regulation cap button.

'A band of olive-drab braid about $1\frac{7}{8}$ inches in width around entire cap.'

Army Air Force Officers' service cap

The same as above except 'front spring stiffening may be omitted and the grommet may be removed.'

Enlisted men's service cap

The same as above 'without band of braid.'

Service hat for all ranks

Made of 'beaver color' felt, it was 'a standard adopted design with "Montana peak", four indentations, crown $5\frac{1}{4}$ inches high for size $7\frac{1}{8}$, with an olive-drab band and bow $\frac{15}{16}$ inch in width. Hat to

This olive green knitted wool sweater was designed to be worn under the M1941 field jacket in cold weather.

be equipped with a leather chinstrap $\frac{5}{8}$ inch in width for officers and $\frac{3}{8}$ inch in width for enlisted men.'

Field jacket for all ranks [i.e., 'M1941' field jacket]

'A six- or seven-button jacket, depending on length, with a two-piece adjustable collar with tab to button, semi-peaked lapels, one-piece back with stitched-on belt (side body to side body) and side plaits; two diagonal inside hanging pockets, slide [i.e. zip] fastener to close front in addition to buttons and buttonholes; adjustable tabs to button at cuff of sleeves and bottom of jacket; on each shoulder a loop of same material as the coat let in at the sleeve head seam and reaching to approximately $\frac{3}{4}$ inch of collar, buttoning at the upper end. Loops to be about $2\frac{1}{2}$ inches in width at lower end and $1\frac{1}{2}$ inches in width at collar end, and cross-stitched down shoulder for a distance of about $1\frac{1}{2}$ inches from lower end. All buttons to be olive-drab 24 ligne.'

Necktie for all ranks

Either khaki or black 'without stripe or figure.'

Service shirt for all ranks

'Of adopted pattern. For officers only, on each shoulder a loop of same material as the shirt let into the sleeve head seam and reaching to the edge of the collar, buttoning at the upper end with a small regulation shirt button. Loops about 2 inches in width at lower end and $1\frac{1}{2}$ inches in width at collar end, and cross-stitched down to shoulder for a distance of 2 inches from lower end.'

Trousers for all ranks

'Of adopted standard, cut on the lines of civilian trousers, without cuffs and without plaits.'

Changes made to AR 600–35, 4 September 1942

Coat, Service, Summer for Officers and Warrant Officers

To be made of khaki gabardine, it was 'a single-breasted semiform-fitting sack coat, extending to crotch, with no pronounced flare or waistline seam. To fit easily over the chest and shoulders and to be fitted slightly at the waist to conform to the figure. The left front to appear straight from top button to bottom of front; buttoned down the front with four large regulation coat buttons equally spaced. Sufficient flare to be on the right front in order to remain underlapped. All buttons to be detachable.

'A vent in the back to extend from immediately below waistline to bottom, following the back seam

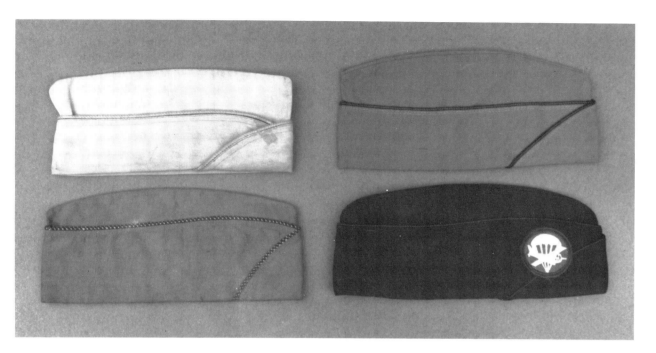

Various examples of overseas caps. Top left: Faded almost to white, a khaki summer-weight enlisted man's cap with sky-blue infantry piping. Top right: The mohair officer's summer cap, with black/gold piping. Bottom left: Enlisted man's summer cap piped in maroon and white, indicating medical personnel. Bottom right: Winter dark shade olive drab officer's cap, with the airborne troops patch authorised in spring 1943—white glider and parachute motif on medium blue disc bordered red. From 1941 until spring 1943 airborne patches were worn on the left side of the cap in sky blue, bearing a white parachute or a white glider for parachute or glider infantry respectively; artillery wore the patch with a red ground. In spring 1943 the new patch, which combined all the airborne arms, replaced these; and officers moved theirs to the right side, to accommodate rank insignia on the left side, although enlisted men continued to wear them on the left.

and with an underlap of approximately $2\frac{1}{2}$ inches.

'The collar to measure approximately $1\frac{5}{8}$ inches in width at the back, the opening between collar end and lapel not to exceed $\frac{1}{2}$ inch. The lapels to be semi-peaked, not wider than $\frac{1}{2}$ inch more than the collar end, and the top edge to be horizontal.

'On each shoulder a loop', as on the winter service coat. The same cuff braid as on the winter coat was also to be worn, and the four pockets were the same as the winter coat.

Officers' overcoat

To the 1941 overcoat was added 'a 36-ligne button placed inside the top left large regulation front button for use in holding right front fly in place.'

Headgear

The Model 1941 knit wool cap for all ranks, 'a standard adopted design with curtain and visor', made of 'olive-drab, wool knit' was added to the list of available headgear: this was the 'beanie', so hated by George Patton.

Necktie for all ranks

Now only to be of 'cotton, mohair, olive-drab, No.3.'

Service shirt

Warrant officers were to wear the officers' pattern shirt with shoulder epaulettes.

Uniforms according to AR 600–35, 31 March 1944 (additions and changes since 1941, 1942)

Service breeches

To match the service coat in colour and material. The materials were wool, elastique, barathea, or whipcord, $14\frac{1}{2}$–26 ounce, while the colour was 'olive-drab shade No.51 (dark shade)'.

The breeches were 'cut snug at the waist, top about 2 inches above hip bone, full in the seat and loose in the thigh, with sufficient length from waist to knee to permit wearer to assume a squatting position without binding at the seat or knee, breeches to present an appearance of fullness when standing; cut right for about 3 inches immediately below the knee and easy for the balance of the length so as not to bind the muscles of the calf. To have a strapping of the same material or buckskin of similar color on the inside of the leg at the knee, extending to a little below the top of the boot and

The olive drab cotton flannel long-sleeved undervest or T-shirt issued for winter wear.

from 6 to 8 inches above the knee.'

Officers' and Warrant Officers' service coat
Basically the same as before, to be made of wool, elastique, barathea, or whipcord, $14\frac{1}{2}$–26 ounce, coloured 'olive-drab shade No.51 (dark shade)'. The back was now 'to be plain'. The bottom button was changed from a regulation gilt button to a 'four-hole 36-ligne button of bone, plastic, or other suitable material of a color closely approximating that of the coat'. This was hidden by 'a matching cloth belt $1\frac{3}{4}$ inches in width having a mitered end and equipped with a $1\frac{3}{4}$-inch tongueless bar buckle with rounded corners, raised polished rims and horizontally lined background of gold color metal $\frac{1}{4}$ inch in width. The belt may be either fully detachable or sewed down around the waistline to a point approximately $2\frac{1}{2}$ inches from the front edge of the coat on each side at the option of the individual. When the belt is detachable, provision will be made for two $\frac{1}{8}$-inch cloth belt loops placed at the side seams sewed on so that they will not mar the coat if removed for a sewed-on belt. The belt will cover the horizontal seam at the waistline and the buckle will be centered over the bottom button of the coat when buttoned. The mitered end of the belt will pass through the buckle to the left, extend not more than 3 inches beyond the buckle, and may be held in place by a cloth keeper $\frac{9}{16}$-inch in width.'

Field jacket for all ranks
The Model 1943 field jacket was to be made of cotton cloth, wind resistant and water repellant, of 'olive-drab shade No.7'. It was 'a coat type jacket, plain back, fly front with six 36-ligne buttons and with adjustable waistline drawcord, body and sleeves lined throughout, with two outside breast cargo type pockets and two lower inside hanging pockets with all straps and concealed buttonhole tabs. Provided with throat tabs with two buttonholes for 30-ligne buttons and shirt cuff type with adjustable sleeve closure. On each shoulder, a loop of the same material as the jacket let in at the sleeve head seam and reaching to the neckband, buttoning at the upper end with a small button. Loops to be about $2\frac{1}{2}$ inches in width at lower edge and $1\frac{1}{2}$ inches in width at upper edge.'

Muffler
'Wool, olive-drab, commercial pattern.'

Necktie for all ranks
To be of a cotton warp, mohair filling fabric coloured in 'khaki shade No.5'.

Officers' and Warrant Officers' long field coat
Made of wind resistant and water repellant cotton poplin or twill 5-ounce cloth, this was available in 'olive-drab shades No.2 and No.7'. It was 'a utility coat, two-ply throughout with a buttoned-in removable wool lining; double breasted with convertible style roll collar and notched lapel, buttoned down the front with a double row of large overcoat buttons, four on each side, with the top buttons approximately 7 inches apart, a diagonal buttonhole placed in lower corner of each front to button to side seams to facilitate marching. A yoke for right shoulder buttoned in front with a 30-ligne button and a throat tab provided with two buttonholes for 30-ligne buttons. Back to be plain with set-in cantle piece closed with a small loop and 30-ligne button. A detachable belt same material as coat with $2\frac{1}{4}$ inches tongueless bar buckle and belt

keeper held in place by two side loops and a strap keeper and belt strap. Adjustable tabs to button at cuff of sleeves.

'Two diagonal hanging pockets, cut hand opening in lining, and finished with pointed flaps buttoning to the rear.

'On each shoulder a loop about 5 inches in length, 2½ inches in width at the lower end, and 1½ inches in width at the upper end which is slightly pointed, the same material as the coat, let in at the sleeve head seam, buttoning at the upper end with a 30-ligne button.'

The lining was 'made from an olive-drab wool fabric with inside yoke extending down 5 inches below armhole, and facing of olive-drab rayon fabric, 14 buttonholes for buttoning into overcoat body. Four buttons are positioned on right front for using as a separate garment. Two large patch pockets with diagonal slash above each pocket in line with openings through coat.'

Officers' and Warrant Officers' short field coat

This coat was coloured 'olive-drab No.51'. It was made from 26–32 ounce beaver, 26–32 ounce doeskin, 26–32 ounce jersey, or 26–32 ounce melton cloth.

The coat was 'a double-breasted coat, lined or unlined, with a notched lapel roll collar approximately 5 inches in width, buttoned down the front with a double row of large regulation buttons, three on each side below the roll of collar with additional buttons or loops so that the coat can be buttoned to the neck'. It had 'two outside patch pockets, one on each side. On each shoulder a loop about 5 inches in length', otherwise the same as on the long overcoat.

'Skirt to extend to 6 inches above the knee. Slit in the back extending about 15 inches from the bottom.' Sleeve decoration was the same as for the 1941 officers' overcoat.

Officers' and Warrant Officers' raincoat

'A coat of commercial pattern, with shoulder loops, color, olive-drab No.7.'

The heavy cotton duck gaiters. The stencilled 'o165K' is the owner's identification number. The other stamp reads 'LEGGINGS, CANVAS, M 1938—DISMOUNTED (O.D.)/ MASCO AWNINGS INC./ 10 20 43 W12 036 QM 130 012830 4 X G/STOCK NO. 72 1 01089/ JEFF. Q.M. DEPOT'.

Identification tags

According to AR 600–35, these were 'of monel metal, approximately 2 inches long by $1\frac{1}{8}$ inches wide, and about $\frac{1}{40}$ inch thick, the corners rounded and the edges smooth. Each tag has a capacity of five lines of type, 18 spaces to the line, and will be embossed by a machine provided for that purpose as follows:

'First line: Name of wearer.

'Second line: First eight spaces, Army serial number; ninth space vacant; tenth, eleventh, and twelfth spaces, record of tetanus immunisation (date completed) (letter T and the last two numerals of the year); thirteenth space vacant; fourteenth and fifteenth spaces, the last two numerals of the year in which the immunity stimulating injection of the tetanus toxoid is completed; sixteenth space vacant; seventeenth space, the letter signifying the blood type; eighteenth space vacant unless the blood type is indicated by two letters. For example: "33333333 space T41 space 42 space A"; or, "33333333 space 41 space 42 space AB". Blood types are indicated by the symbols "A", "B", "AB", or "O".

'Third line: Name of person to be notified in case of emergency.

'Fourth line: Street address of person to be notified in case of emergency.

One type of winter boot, the feet made of black rubber attached to a lace-up leather upper.

'Fifth line: City and State address of person to be notified in case of emergency.

'The religion of the wearer, when stated, will be stamped in space 18 of the fifth line if that space is vacant, otherwise in space 18 of the fourth line, and will be indicated by a capital letter as follows: C for Catholic; H for Hebrew; and P for Protestant.'

The name and address of a person to be notified in case of emergency was eliminated with the 31 March 1944 copy of AR 600–35.

The tags were to be worn around the neck 'by a cord or tape 40 inches in length passed through one small hole in the tag, the second tag to be fastened about $2\frac{1}{2}$ inches above the first one on the same cord or tape, both securely held in place by knots', according to Circular 262, War Department, 19 December 1941. 'These tags are prescribed as part of the uniform and will be habitually worn by the owner.'

The issue combat boot, made with the russet brown leather 'rough side out', and soles of black rubber with white cords running through them for added strength.

Insignia

According to Army Regulation 600–35, 10 November 1941

General

a. Except as otherwise prescribed, insignia for wear upon uniform clothing will be made of gold or gold color metal.

b. Elements superimposed on insignia of officers, except as otherwise prescribed, will be of bronze finish or brown enamel.

c. Elements superimposed on insignia of enlisted men will be of the same material as the insignia.

d. Certain insignia which involve the use of heads will be made to face to dexter.

e. Metal insignia will have screw backs or similar attachments so that they will be held closely without turning or flopping.

f. Insignia of grade for shoulder loops may be embroidered.

g. Metal insignia of grade may be knurled or smooth.

Insignia and ornamentation for headgear—a. Cap, garrison:

(1) Ornamentation:

(*a*) *General officers*—Cord edge braid of gold bullion or metallised cellophane of gold color.

(*b*) *Other officers*—Cord edge braid of gold bullion or metallised cellophane of gold color and black silk intermixed.

(*c*) *Warrant officers*—Cord edge braid of silver bullion or metallised cellophane of silver color and black silk intermixed.

(*d*) *Enlisted men*—Cord edge braid of the color of arm, service, or bureau.

Insignia of grade.—a. Officers

(1) *General*—Four silver stars 1 inch in diameter.

(2) *Lieutenant general*—Three silver stars 1 inch in diameter.

(3) *Major general*—Two silver stars 1 inch in diameter.

(4) *Brigadier general*—One silver star 1 inch in diameter.

(5) *Colonel*—A silver spread eagle $\frac{3}{4}$ inch in height and $1\frac{1}{2}$ inches between tips of wings. Insignia to be made in pairs so, when worn, head of eagle will face to the front.

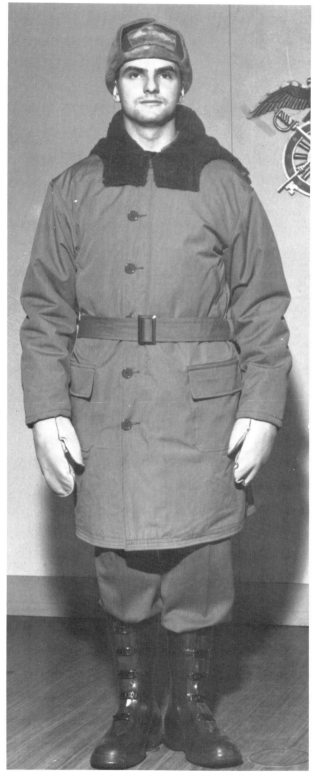

This coat, first issued in 1941, was made of two-ply cotton lined with alpaca pile fabric in the body and hood; sleeves were wool-lined, and the hood had a slide fastener in the centre for opening and closing. (US Army)

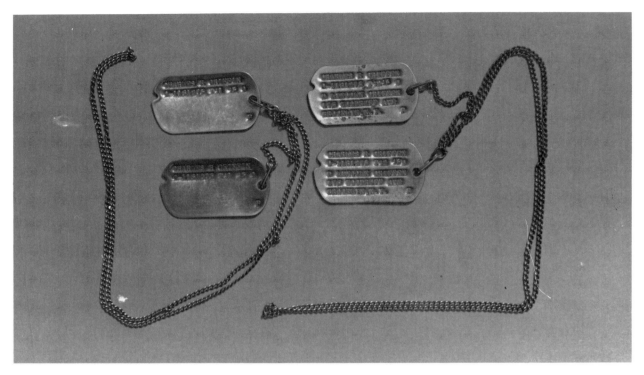

Identification tags: right, 1941 style, and left, 1944 style without name and address of next of kin. The wearer's serial number on this example has an 'O' prefix, indicating an officer.

(6) *Lieutenant colonel*—A silver oak leaf 1 inch in height and 1 inch across.

(7) *Major*—A gold oak leaf 1 inch in height and 1 inch across.

(8) *Captain*—Two silver bars each $\frac{3}{8}$ inch in width and 1 inch in length. Bars to be $\frac{1}{4}$ inch apart.

(9) *First lieutenant*—One silver bar $\frac{3}{8}$ inch in width and 1 inch in length.

(10) *Second lieutenant*—One gold bar $\frac{3}{8}$ inch in width and 1 inch in length.

b. Warrant officers, Army Mine Planter Service

(1) *Master*—Four bands of brown braid $\frac{1}{2}$ inch in width and an embroidered brown foul anchor 1 inch in length for each sleeve.

(2) *Chief engineer*—Four bands of brown braid $\frac{1}{2}$ inch in width and an embroidered brown three-bladed propeller 1 inch in diameter for each sleeve.

(3) *First mate*—Three bands of brown braid $\frac{1}{2}$ inch in width and an embroidered brown foul anchor 1 inch in length for each sleeve.

(4) *Assistant engineer*—Three bands of brown braid $\frac{1}{2}$ inch in width and an embroidered brown three-bladed propeller 1 inch in diameter for each sleeve.

(5) *Second assistant engineer*—Two bands of brown braid $\frac{1}{2}$ inch in width and an embroidered brown three-bladed propeller 1 inch in diameter for each sleeve.

(6) *Second mate*—Two bands of brown braid $\frac{1}{2}$ inch in width and an embroidered brown foul anchor 1 inch in length for each sleeve.

[Other warrant officers were marked only by their coat lapel and cap insignia.]

d. Enlisted men

(1) Non-commissioned officers and first class privates will have insignia of grade on a background forming an edging around the entire insignia and between each chevron, as follows:

(*a*) Cotton, khaki chevrons, arcs, and lozenge on a dark blue cotton background.

(*b*) Olive-drab wool chevrons, arcs, and lozenge on a dark blue wool background.

(2) *Master sergeant (first grade)*—Three chevrons and an arc of three bars, the upper bar of arc forming a tie to the lower chevron.

(3) *Technical sergeant (second grade)*—Three chevrons and an arc of two bars, the upper bar of arc forming a tie to the lower chevron.

(4) *First sergeant (second grade)*—Three chevrons and an arc of two bars, the upper bar of arc forming a tie to the lower chevron. In the angle between

16

lower chevrons and upper bar, a hollow lozenge.

(5) *Staff sergeant (third grade)*—Three chevrons and an arc of one bar forming a tie to the lower chevron.

(6) *Sergeant (fourth grade)*—Three chevrons.

(7) *Corporal (fifth grade) and acting corporal*—Two chevrons.

(8) *First class private (sixth grade)*—One chevron.

Brassards

All brassards to be of cloth 18 inches in length and 4 inches in width of the color specified. When the brassard consists of more than one color, the colors will be of equal width and will run lengthwise of the brassard.

(a) *General Staff Corps*—The letters 'G.S.C.' in rounded block type 1 inch in height to be placed in the center of the brassard. The colors for the various

headquarters will be as follows:

(1) *Divisions*—Red with white letters.

(2) *Army corps and corps areas*—Blue and white, blue uppermost, with red letters.

(3) *Armies*—White and red, white uppermost, with blue letters.

(4) *Headquarters of field forces and War Department*—Blue, white and red in order from top to bottom, with blue letters.

(b) *Military police*—The letters 'M.P.' in block type in white $2\frac{1}{2}$ inches in height on a dark blue background.

(c) *All persons in the military service rendered neutral by the terms of the Geneva Convention in time of war*—A red Geneva cross on a white background.

(d) *Men on recruiting duty*—The words 'Recruiting

A representative group of left shoulder insignia; the soldier would wear that of the smallest organisation to which his immediate unit belonged—division, corps, army, theatre of operations, etc. These are, from left to right: *Top row:* Pacific Theatre of Operations—white and red on blue; European Theatre of Operations, advanced base—blue star on white, red flashes, yellow details, on blue; Middle Eastern Theatre of Operations—blue star on white, red edge. *Second row:* 1st Army—black on white and red; XXI Corps—red and white on blue shamrock on olive; Officer's Candidate School—olive on black. *Third row:* 46th Infantry Division—yellow on blue; American Division, white on blue. *Bottom row:* 7th Army—red and yellow on blue; Airborne Command—white on red shield below yellow on black title; 4th Army—white on red.

Service' in white block letters 1 inch in height on a dark blue background.

(*e*) *Members of fire truck and hose companies*—The word 'Fire' in white block letters 2¼ inches in height on a red background.

(*f*) *Port officers*—The letters 'A.T.S.' in black 1¼ inches in height, followed immediately below by designation of position of department, as provided in AR 30–115, on a buff background.

(*g*) *Members of veterinary service*—A green cross on a white background.

(*h*) *Newspaper correspondents, photographers, and broadcasters attached to and authorised to accompany forces of the Army of the United States in the theater of operations and their chauffeurs and messengers*—The appropriate title, 'Correspondent,' 'Photographer,' 'Radio Commentator,' 'Correspondent Chauffeur,' 'Photographer Chauffeur,' 'Correspondent Messenger,' 'Photographer Messenger,' or 'Radio News Messenger,' in white block letters 1¼ inches in height on a green background.

Changes and additions of 4 September 1942

c. Warrant officers other than that of the Army Mine Planter Service

(1) *Chief warrant officer*—One gold bar ⅜ inch in width and 1 inch in length, with rounded ends, having a brown enameled top and a longitudinal center of gold ⅛ inch in width.

(2) *Warrant officer (junior grade)*—One gold bar ⅜ inch in width and 1 inch in length, with rounded ends, having a brown enameled top and a latitudinal center of gold ⅛ inch in width.

d. Enlisted men

(6) *Technician (third grade)*—Three chevrons and an arc of one bar forming a tie to the lower chevron. In the angle between lower chevrons and bar a letter T.

(7) *Sergeant (fourth grade)*—Three chevrons.

(8) *Technician (fourth grade)*—Three chevrons above a letter T.

(9) *Corporal (fifth grade) and acting corporal*—Two chevrons.

(10) *Technician (fifth grade)*—Two chevrons above a letter T.

Brassards

h. Newspaper correspondents, photographers, and broadcasters attached to and authorised to accompany forces of the Army of the United States in the theater of operations:

A warrant officer (junior grade) in summer dress; note the insignia of this rank worn on the shoulder loops and the shirt collar points. Cap piping would be silver and black.

(1) Journalists, feature writers, and radio commentators—A white block letter 'C' 2 inches in height on a green background.

(2) Photographers—A white block letter 'P' 2 inches in height on a green background.

j. Civilian employees in forces of the Army of the United States in theater of operations having a status recognised by the War Department as part of the forces:

Emblem, sleeve, noncombatant—For civilian employees in forces of the Army of the United States, having a status recognised by the War Department as part of the forces, and civilian personnel of all United States military missions in theaters of operations and overseas garrisons, an emblem of dark blue cloth, 4½ inches in width, 4½ inches in height, charged with a white equilateral triangle with the letters 'US' in dark blue, 1½ inches in width and 1½ inches in height, thereon.

Insignia, officer candidate school—On a dark-blue cloth background, 2¼ inches in diameter, the letters 'CS'

Army Branch Colours and Insignia

Branch	Colour	Insignia
Adjutant General's Department	Dark blue piped with scarlet (white until March 1944)*	Dark blue shield
Air Force	Ultra marine piped golden orange	Wings and propeller
Armoured Units	Green piped with white	Tank
Cavalry	Yellow	Crossed sabres
Chaplains	Black*	Latin cross (Christian) Double tables and interlaced triangles (Jewish)
Chemical Warfare Service	Cobalt blue piped golden yellow	Benzol ring and crossed retorts
Coast Artillery	Scarlet	Crossed cannon and projectile in red oval
Detached Enlisted Men's List	Green	Arms of the United States
Engineer Corps	Scarlet piped white	Castle
Field Artillery	Scarlet	Crossed cannon
Finance Department	Silver gray piped golden yellow	Diamond
Infantry	Light blue	Crossed rifles
Inspector General's Department	Dark blue piped light blue (white until March 1944)*	Crossed swords and fasces and a wreath
Judge Advocate General's Department	Dark blue piped with white (light blue until March 1944)*	Crossed sword and pen wreathed
Medical Department	Maroon piped white	Caduceus
Military Intelligence Reserve	Golden yellow piped with purple	Sphinx within a circle within an eared shield
Military Police	Yellow piped with green	Crossed pistols
Militia Bureau	Dark blue	Crossed fasces and eagle
Ordnance Department	Crimson piped with yellow	Shell and flame
Permanent professors of the US Military Academy (USMA)	Scarlet piped with silver gray*	USMA coat of arms
Quartermaster Corps	Buff	Eagle surmounting wheel with crossed sword and key
Signal Corps	Orange and white	Crossed signal flags with flaming torch
Specialist Reserve	Brown piped with golden yellow*	Arms of the United States
Tank Destroyer Units	Golden-orange and black	M3 self-propelled gun
Transportation Corps	Brick red with golden yellow	Winged car wheel on a shield on a ship's wheel
Warrant Officers	Brown*	Rising eagle within a wreath
Woman's Army Corps	Old gold piped with moss-tone green	Head of Athena

* Colours seen only as officers' dress uniform trim—all-officer branch.

The M1 steel helmet. The vertical white bar painted at the rear indicates a commissioned officer; the white disc at the sides is the unit marking of the 101st Airborne Division's artillery component. Such unit flashes were not common in the field.

combatant—For civilian employees in forces of the Army of the United States, having a status recognised by the War Department as part of the forces, and civilian personnel of all United States military missions in theaters of operations and overseas garrisons, a sleeve emblem, as follows:
a. Combatant—For personnel who are required to perform combatant duties, an emblem of dark blue cloth, $4\frac{1}{2}$ inches in width, $4\frac{1}{2}$ inches in height, charged with a scarlet equilateral triangle with the letters 'US' in dark blue, $1\frac{1}{2}$ inches in width and $1\frac{1}{2}$ inches in height, thereon.
b. Noncombatant—For all other personnel, as in *a* above, except that the triangle will be white.
Insignia, bomb disposal personnel—On a black projectile shape, point downward, $1\frac{7}{16}$ inches in width by $2\frac{3}{4}$ inches in length, a red conventionalised drop bomb fimbriated in yellow $\frac{7}{8}$ inch in width by $2\frac{3}{8}$ inches in length.

in monogram form, within the letter 'O' in olive-drab, all elements $\frac{5}{32}$ inch in width.

Changes and Additions of 31 March 1944

Insignia of grade—a. Officers

c. Flight officer—One gold bar $\frac{3}{8}$ inch in width and 1 inch in length, with rounded ends, having a blue enameled top and a latitudinal center of gold $\frac{1}{8}$ inch in width.

d. Enlisted men

(3) *First sergeant (first grade)*—Three chevrons and an arc of three bars, the upper bar of arc forming a tie to the lower chevron. In the angle between the lower chevrons and upper bar, a hollow lozenge. Insignia to denote excellence, Army Specialised Training Program—On an olive-drab disc, a blue star 1 inch in diameter.

Brassards

i. Technical observers and service specialists accompanying United States Army forces in field—The letters TO in black $1\frac{1}{4}$ inches in height on an orange background.
k. Gas personnel—The letters 'GAS' in golden yellow letters $2\frac{1}{2}$ inches in height on a cobalt blue background.
l. Auxiliary military police—The words 'AUXILIARY MILITARY POLICE' in blue letters $\frac{3}{4}$ inch in height on a white background.
Emblem, sleeve, combatant, and emblem, sleeve, non-

Personal Equipment

Combat Headgear

In 1942 the M1 helmet and liner was introduced into the US Army. It was made of steel, with web chinstraps fastened by a claw-like metal double hook on the left side which snapped around an 'arrowhead' tongue in a buckle on the right side. The chinstrap in the European Theatre of Operations was usually tucked up on the rear rim of the helmet away from the chin: if left dangling it could catch into the field jacket epaulette. The helmet was painted olive green shade No.7 in a paint and sand mixture, giving the finish a dull appearance for camouflage purposes.

Airborne units wore the M1C version, identical except for additional web A-straps attached to the liner, to which was buckled a leather chin cup. The cup was sometimes discarded during ground combat, and the thin web A-straps tucked up inside the liner.

The helmet liner was made of a lightweight compressed fibre, painted the same colour as the helmet on the outside, and had a striped brown or green and black finish inside. It fitted snugly to the head by means of a set of thin leather sweat bands adjusted by metal clips to the web belting permanently arranged in the liner. Officers officially had a special style helmet liner, with a thicker rim and a fabric finish; but these were rarely seen in any of the combat areas. The helmet liner was widely worn by itself for parade use. Officers wore their rank badges on the fronts of helmet liners, and often unit insignia were painted on them.

Helmet shells were often marked, too. Military police usually had block letters 'MP' painted on the front, while medical personnel had red Geneva crosses painted on all four sides. In the Pacific unit markings and sometimes rank insignia were painted on the backs or sides of the helmets, but not on the front. Officers' rank badges were often required to be painted or affixed to the fronts of helmets in the European Theatre of Operations, especially in Gen. Patton's command. It was also common in various commands in the ETO for the back of helmets to be marked with a vertical white stripe for a commissioned officer and a horizontal white stripe for a non-commissioned officer. Some units in the ETO also placed their distinctive insignia on the sides of their helmets, but this was rare in combat zones.

The helmet gave poor protection from cold weather, even though it was excellent protection in combat; and various extra types of headgear were worn with it in severe weather.

The first was the M1941 wool knit cap. This had a 'curtain' flap at the sides and rear which could be

The M1910 haversack, showing maker's markings and date.

The M1923 rifle belt, marked 'U.S.' on the right front hip pouch, and dated inside 1943. Note how it can be adjusted to fit by an inside belt. The open pouch shows a clip retainer.

worn down over the ears when needed, or left folded up. It also had a small peak in front. For even colder weather an olive drab wool knitted toque, a sort of 'Balaclava helmet', was issued. These were often made by civilian volunteer knitters and varied tremendously in exact shade and style, as well as type of wool. Their use was uncommon.

With the introduction of the M1943 field jacket came the M1944 hood. This was made of the same material as the jacket, a treated cotton, and buttoned on around the jacket collar. It was cut quite large so that it could actually fit over the helmet, buttoning snugly under the chin. Because it restricted hearing and head movement it was not very popular among front line combat troops, although support troops who were still required to wear helmets used their M1944 hoods widely. The hood could also be worn under the helmet.

In the ETO dark green string netting coverings were usually worn over helmets for additional camouflage. When needed, leaves and small branches could be inserted into them, but this was not commonly done. These coverings were rarely seen in the Pacific.

The M1 helmet was one of the most successful pieces of equipment introduced in the Army during the Second World War. Not only did it provide excellent protection for the head, neck and ears, but because the helmet and liner were separate the helmet shell itself could be used as a wash basin, a water-carrier, or for various other front-line chores.

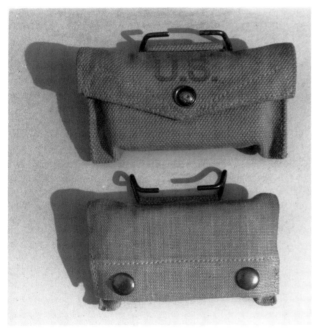

Both these types of first aid pouch were widely used. The top one is marked 'M.W. CO. LTD. 1944/BRITISH MADE'; the lower one, 'THE M-H CO./ 7–1918', indicating manufacture in July 1918.

Field Equipment

The basic combat infantryman's load was developed and later modified in 1910. It included a cartridge belt with pockets, each one holding two five-round clips of rifle ammunition; a haversack; a pack carrier; a canteen and cup within a cover; and a set of mess gear within a pack. A bayonet scabbard and bayonet and an entrenching tool within its cover could be carried either on the cartridge belt or on the haversack. The haversack was carried on braces with the combat pack, which also included the mess gear pouch (known as the 'meat can and pouch'), the bayonet and scabbard, the entrenching tool and cover, and a first aid packet on the belt. A complete pack included all this, with a pack carrier holding a roll with blankets and spare clothing within a shelter half.

The Model 1936 field bag, usually called a 'musette bag', was carried as part of this equipment by officers and mechanised troops. Because of its relative inflexibility, the Model 1910 'long pack' was replaced with a Model 1944 cargo pack, a Model 1945 combat pack, and a pack originally designed for jungle use but later designated the Model 1943 field pack.

With the introduction of the M1 rifle, which held an eight-round clip, some changes had to be made to the cartridge belt. The Model 1923 belt, changed from the Model 1910 belt in only minor ways, was found to hold 80 rounds of M1 ammunition in clips, and so was the most common cartridge belt of the war. It was made with retaining straps for the clips within the pouches, although these do not seem to have been put into American-made M1923 belts after 1943. British-made M1923 belts dated as late as 1945 still have them.

However, in 1938 a modified M1923 cartridge belt, the M1938 belt, was introduced. It is the same as the earlier belt except that the pouches are made narrower so that one more pouch could be squeezed into each side. The M1938 belt therefore had a 96-round capacity, in the unmounted version. The mounted version had an 88-round capacity and a pouch for two .45 automatic pistol ammunition clips.

In late 1944 the colour of all web field gear was officially ordered changed from khaki to olive-green, Shade No.7.

A special 'landing' or 'assault' pack was issued to designated units making the D-Day invasion landing in Normandy: these included the 16th and 18th Infantry Regiments of the 1st Infantry Division and the 116th Infantry Regiment, 29th Infantry Division. These packs were made in the form of a waistcoat, with four large pockets in the front and two large pouches in the back, one on the square of the back and the smaller one below the waistline. The pack was issued in the staging areas in England just prior to the invasion and, because of its great unpopularity, was abandoned by virtually all wearers two or three days after landing.

The first aid packet was modified so that the cover, which used to cover the entire front and was fastened with two snaps, was replaced with a V-shaped cover shut with only one snap in the centre of the packet. Both styles were seen throughout the war.

The aluminium cap of the canteen was replaced by 1942 with a black plastic model. Again, due to vast supplies remaining from 1918, both styles were seen throughout the war.

The rifle cartridge belt was felt to be unsatisfactory by some troops, and many men, including infantry riflemen, preferred using light-weight, olive-green cotton clip-pouch bandoliers slung around the neck. Instead of the cartridge belt they wore a Model 1912 web pistol belt, made with eyelets through which the various other pieces of equipment—such as the canteen, first aid packet and entrenching tool cover—could be hooked. The M1912 web pistol belt was also worn as issue equipment by all officers, senior non-commissioned officers, and enlisted men whose positions called for the use of a pistol or carbine instead of a rifle, such as drivers or photographers. According to paragraph 61, AR 600–40, the standard field equipment for officers included the M1912 web pistol belt, the M1936 suspenders, and the M1936 canvas field bag. Whitened pistol belts were worn by MPs in the European theatre.

Troops on manoeuvres in Australia in March 1943, displaying typical tropical field dress. Shirts are worn outside the trousers with rolled sleeves, and trousers are not always tucked into leggings. (US Army)

When the pistol was issued it was carried in a russet leather holster on the right hip. Two spare clips of ammunition were carried in the ammunition pouch worn on the left front hip. This was an unusual item among the issue web equipment, in that it did not hook to the belt, but was made with a wide web loop at the back which slid over the belt.

All web equipment, and the leather pistol holster, were visibly marked with the block letters 'U.S.'; web gear markings were in black, while the holster was stamped with the letters within an oval. All web

The M1936 officer's field bag, or 'musette bag', with a stencilled marking showing the officer's name and O-prefix serial.

The M1912 pistol belt, showing how it can be adjusted for size.

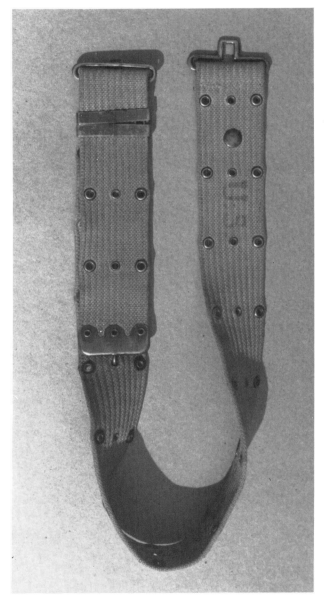

gear was marked with the maker's name and date of manufacture inside pouch flaps or belts where it would not be visible when the equipment was worn.

The gas mask, rarely carried in the field in Europe or the Pacific, was carried separately from the other web equipment in its own large pouch slung on the left side.

Special types of web gear, still conforming to the general principles of the 1910 equipment, were issued to troops needing them. For example, special large bags similar to the M1936 field bag were issued to field Medical Corps personnel. Among other types of equipment issued were ammunition pouches for the M1922 Browning Automatic Rifle, M1928 Thompson sub-machine gun, M1 carbine and M3 sub-machine gun. These pouches, needed quickly in combat zones, were not only made in the United States, but by British and Australian makers as well. The snaps used on American-made equipment differ from those made by foreign makers, however.

Infantry Weapons

M1 Rifle: Although the old '03 Springfield bolt-action rifle saw use early in the war, the standard

1: Lt. Col., General Staff; USA, 1941
2: Tech. Sgt., 9th Inf., 2nd Inf. Div.; USA, 1941
3: 2nd Lt., mounted branch; USA, 1941

A

1: PFC, Ordnance Corps; Pacific Theatre, late 1941
2: Master Sgt., 59th Coast Arty.; USA, 1941
3: Major, 4th Eng., 4th Inf. Div.; USA, 1941
4: Col., 2nd Cav., 2nd Cav. Div.; N. Africa, 1944

B

1: 1st Sgt., 28th Inf. Div.; USA, 1942-43
2: 1st Lt., 8th Inf. Div.; USA, 1942
3: Cpl., 1st Cav. Div.; USA, 1942

C

1: Sgt., 45th Inf. Div.; N. Africa, 1943
2: Tech. 4th Grade, 51st Sigs. Corps; France, 1944
3: Brig. Gen., Services of Supply, 1942

D

Private, US Cavalry; USA, 1942

E

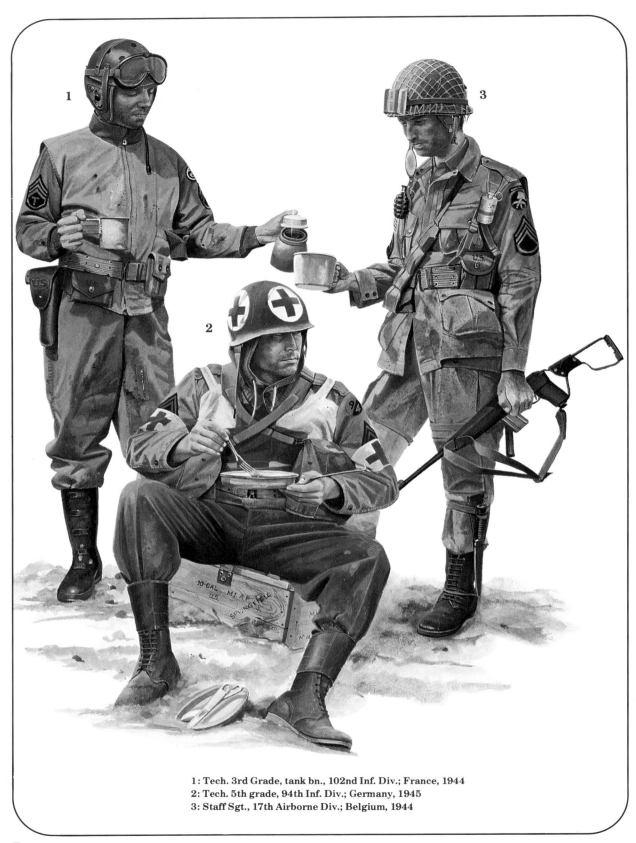

1: Tech. 3rd Grade, tank bn., 102nd Inf. Div.; France, 1944
2: Tech. 5th grade, 94th Inf. Div.; Germany, 1945
3: Staff Sgt., 17th Airborne Div.; Belgium, 1944

F

1: PFC, Alamo Scouts, 6th Army; Pacific Theatre, 1944
2: 2nd Lt., 81st Inf. Div.; Pacific Theatre, 1944
3: Pte., 17th Armd. Eng. Bn., 2nd Armd. Div.: Normandy, 1944

1: Tech. 5th Grade, MP Co., III Corps; Germany, 1945
2: 1st Sgt., 1st Special Service Force; Europe, 1944
3: Capt., 32nd Armor, 3rd Armd. Div.; Germany, 1945

H

infantry weapon from 1942 onwards was the Garand M1 semi-automatic, gas-operated rifle. This .30cal. weapon was 43.6ins long, weighed 9.5lbs, and had a muzzle velocity of 2805fps.; it proved a reliable and accurate rifle, and served the GI well. Its effective range was at least 500 yards, and its rate of fire was as fast as the rifleman could pull the trigger. It had a non-detachable eight-round magazine, into which 'en bloc' clips were inserted; the cartridges—and, after the eighth shot, the clip itself—were ejected automatically. (The noise made by the clip hitting the ground could be a disadvantage to infantrymen fighting at close range, since it revealed that they had to reload.)

M1911A1 Automatic Pistol: The classic .45cal. 'Colt auto' pistol, in use since before the First World War and much sought after by GIs as a personal 'weapon of last resort', was officially issued to junior leaders and vehicle crews. It was a conventional recoil-operated semi-automatic pistol, taking seven rounds in a detachable magazine; length was 8.62ins, weight 2.43lbs, and muzzle velocity 830fps. Inaccurate at any but the shortest ranges, it had

considerable 'stopping-power' in hand-to-hand combat.

M1 Carbine: The day of the pistol on the battlefield was felt to be almost over, and this .30cal. carbine, based in some respects on the M1 rifle, was issued during the war as a superior alternative for those officers, NCOs and crewmen who carried pistols. It was a gas-operated, semi-automatic weapon, only 35.6ins long and weighing just 5.5lbs; muzzle velocity was 1970fps. Handy and attractive, it was at first popular with any infantryman who could scrounge one; but in combat the short effective range and very limited impact of its cartridge, much shorter and less powerful than rifle ammunition, proved to be a disadvantage. It was, indeed, an 'alternative pistol', not an 'alternative rifle'. The folding-stock M1A1 version was issued to para-

Both types of canteen saw widespread use; the centre one actually dates from before the war, while wartime examples were made with black plastic caps to save metal. This example bears the maker's stamp 'A.G.M. Co./1942', and the owner has personally engraved it with a U.S. cypher, his name, and where he served. Beneath it is the canteen cup, the handle folded to fit inside the canteen pouch, far right.

Vehicle and armoured crews and flying personnel often wore these all-leather shoulder holsters, as worn by the technical sergeant on the right, in place of the standard waistbelt holster, left.

The back surface of the issue holster for the M1912 pistol belt, made of russet-brown leather; note slits, so that it could be used on an ordinary leather belt if needed. It is marked 'MILWAUKEE SADDLERY CO./1944.'

troopers; and at the end of the war some examples of the fully-automatic M2, with a 30-round 'banana' magazine replacing the M1's 15-round detachable straight box type, reached the Pacific.

M1928A1 & M1 Thompson Sub-Machine Gun: The US Army issued sub-machine guns on a more lavish scale than other armies. The squad leader's weapon for most of the war was the classic 'Tommy gun', in several slightly differing versions. This delayed-blowback weapon had a selective fire capability, and put out around 725rpm on full automatic; length was 33.7ins, weight 10.75lbs, and muzzle velocity 920fps. Its practical range was not much more than 100 yards, but in street-fighting or jungle this was adequate, and the .45cal. round had tremendous stopping-power. Both 50-round drum and 20- and 30-round box magazines were used.

M3 Sub-Machine Gun: A mass-produced alternative to the Thompson was introduced late in the war, and nicknamed 'Grease gun' from its stubby, utilitarian appearance. Cheaply made out of steel pressings, the M3 was a .45cal. blowback-operated gun weighing 7.15lbs and measuring only 29.8ins long—seven inches less with its skeleton butt retracted. It had a straight 30-round box magazine; and in its improved M3A1 version it was cocked simply by putting a finger into a hole in the exposed side of the bolt and pulling it back. Muzzle velocity was 920fps, and rate of fire up to 450rpm.

M1922 Browning Automatic Rifle: At squad level the standard light automatic support weapon was the BAR, a gas-operated, selective-fire, .30cal. rifle with a 20-round detachable box magazine. Length was 41ins, weight 19.2lbs, and muzzle velocity around 2700fps; rate of fire on full automatic was 550rpm.

M1919A4 Browning Machine Gun: Normally seen at infantry company level, this air-cooled version of the belt-fed .30cal. Browning machine gun was 41ins long and weighed 31lbs, plus another 14lbs for the M2 tripod mounting. Its muzzle velocity was 2800fps and its rate of fire up to 550rpm. The M1919A6 modification had an added shoulder stock and a bipod mount. Effective range was up to a mile.

The Plates

A1: Lieutenant-colonel, General Staff; United States, 1941
The officer's service uniform was of dark olive drab, although trousers of a light shade, known as 'pinks', could also be worn with this cap and coat. The russet-brown M1921 'Sam Browne' belt was worn until 1943, officially, although it was often abandoned before that date. On 26 November 1942 a belt of the same material as the coat, with a brass buckle, was authorised to be sewn to the waist of the

coat, replacing the Sam Browne, which was forbidden from 7 June 1943.

This officer wears the insignia of the General Staff on his lower lapels. The silver oak leaves of this rank are worn on both shoulder straps. He wears the silver qualification wings of a balloon pilot on the left breast, above ribbons for service on the Mexican Border, in the 2nd Nicaraguan campaign, and for National Defense: the latter was awarded for US Army service in a period just prior to America's official entry into the war.

His embroidered left shoulder patch indicates assignment to the General Headquarters of the US Army. The large enamelled metal insignia on the right breast pocket is a War Department General Staff Identification, authorised for officers who had served for not less than a year, at any time since 4 June 1920, on the War Department General Staff. After 1 March 1942 it could be worn by anyone who served on the General Staff if awarded by the Secretary of War or Assistant Chief of Staff.

Both one-piece (centre) and two-piece camouflage-printed combat fatigues are worn in this photo of US infantry on Bougainville in winter 1943: these may be men of the 3rd Marine or the 37th Infantry divisions. Very light personal equipment is carried, and trousers flap loose at the ankle; note also cotton clip bandoliers slung round the centre soldier—the most popular and practical way to carry rifle ammunition. (US Army)

The two-piece camouflage-printed fatigues in use in the European theatre of Operations: engineers photographed in the front line at Canisy in Normandy in June 1944. The experiment was short-lived. (US Army)

The mess kit, officially called a 'meat can', included a knife, fork, and a spoon (not shown); the spoon and fork were similar in design, while the knife had a black plastic handle, this one marked 'U.S.' on one side and 'L.F.&C./1941' on the other. The handle of the 'meat can' is stamped 'U.S./THE HAMLIN METAL PROD. CO./1942'.

A2: Technical Sergeant, 9th Infantry, 2nd Infantry Division; United States, 1941

Obviously a First World War veteran, this man holds the second highest non-commissioned officer's pay grade, indicated by the chevrons on both upper sleeves. His embroidered left shoulder patch identifies the 2nd Infantry Division, while the gilt badges on each lower lapel identify the 9th Infantry Regiment, assigned to that formation. His upper lapel insignia carry 'U.S.' above '9' on his right, and the crossed-rifles infantry branch badge on his left. His ribbons include a Silver Star, awarded for bravery; a Purple Heart, for suffering a wound; and the rainbow ribbon of the First World War Victory Medal. Under them is pinned an Expert's Badge, the top shooting award, with clasps for Pistol and Rifle.

The small chevron on the right forearm is a First World War wound stripe. The three on the left forearm indicate completed terms of enlistment; the bottom one, edged buff, indicates National Guard service, presumably in the period between the World Wars. The gold chevron worn above these service stripes indicates six months' overseas service in the First World War.

The lanyard is a French *fourragère* in the green and red of the Croix de Guerre ribbon, representing

two citations; this was awarded to the 9th Infantry by the French government for First World War service.

On 10 November 1941 the leather garrison belt was eliminated from the uniform, as were the white shirt and black tie; these were replaced by either an olive drab or a khaki shirt and a khaki tie.

The 2nd Infantry Division was to land in Normandy on 7 June 1944; fighting their way across Europe, they reached the German-Czech

The armoured force winter field uniform posed for official photographs of record: the 'tanker's jacket' with knitted wrists, collar and waistband worn over thickly lined overtrousers cut high to the chest and attaching to adjustable shoulder braces. Flyer's-type gloves were issued, and rubber overshoes. (US Army)

border by VE-Day, their last action being the capture of Pilsen.

A3: Second Lieutenant; United States, 1941
The short overcoat for commissioned officers was first authorised in 1926. It could be worn only on military bases, and not for ceremonies or official duties; and if the troops were dressed in their long overcoats, the officers had to follow suit. However, the short overcoat could be worn in the field or when mounted, and it was ideal for riding; and this officer's riding breeches and boots indicate service with a mounted branch, either cavalry or field artillery. The branch is not otherwise identified, since only rank insignia—here, the gold bar of second lieutenant—are worn on the coat. On 3 April 1943 a new-style short overcoat was authorised, virtually the same as this pattern but with notched lapels and without the cloth waist belt. Unit shoulder patches were authorised for the new coat; and when worn by general officers it bore two black worsted braid bands around each cuff.

B1: Private First Class, Ordnance Corps; Pacific Theatre of Operations, late 1941
The Army's khaki 'chino' shirt and trousers were designed originally to serve both as summer service dress and field uniform. In actual practice it saw service as a field uniform only in the Pacific Theatre and in exercises in the United States early in the war, being replaced by specialised combat uniforms.

Rank chevrons were embroidered in khaki, bordered in dark blue; one chevron identified Private First Class (PFC). Originally the gilt collar discs bearing 'U.S.' and the appropriate branch badge on right and left respectively were worn on the shirt; the insignia of the Ordnance Corps was a flaming bomb. In the new Army dress regulations of 10 November 1941 no mention was made of collar insignia, and they were generally omitted in the field.

Equipment stocks, both in the Pacific and the United States, were fairly obsolete in 1941. Rifles were frequently the old Model 1903 Springfield of the First World War, and the long bayonet was frogged on the left hip. Ammunition was carried in khaki web rifle belts supported by braces, with a canteen at left rear and a first aid packet at right

A rather more realistic study of the front-line use of the same uniform is provided by this 'candid snap' of M7 Priest crewmen of the 274th Armd.Fld.Arty.Bn., 3rd Armd.Div. in the Ardennes during early January 1945. The wool 'beanie' is worn under the fabric 'flyer's' helmet issued for cold-weather wear beneath the leather tank crew helmet. The bib-fronted overtrousers are worn over the tanker's jacket. To fit the rubber overshoes actually on top of leather boots required an enormous size; many men simply wore them as conventional boots, over several pairs of socks. (US Army)

rear. Olive drab leggings were worn over the dull-finished russet boots in the field. Steel helmets were of the old 1918 pattern copied from the British model, painted dark olive drab.

B2: Master Sergeant, 59th Coast Artillery; United States, 1941
The Coast Artillery Corps had the task of attacking enemy naval vessels with artillery and submarine mines, and enemy aircraft with A/A fire.

The campaign hat was the standard field headgear in the United States except among

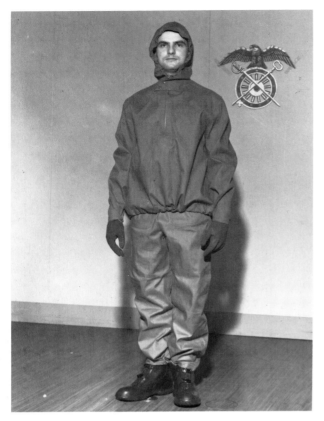

armoured and airborne troops, who wore the flat overseas cap. The distinctive regimental insignia was pinned to the front in enamelled metal form; the hat cords were in corps colours, in this case scarlet. The regimental number appears below the national cypher on the right collar disc, while the left disc bears the corps insignia of a shell on an oval cartouche on crossed cannon; the cartouche was white, edged with red, on officer's insignia. The sleeve chevrons identify the grade of master sergeant, the highest NCO grade in the Army.

B3: Major, 4th Engineers, 4th Infantry Division; United States, 1941

The overseas cap, worn in France in 1917–18, was then abandoned until 22 August 1933, when it was revived for use by tank and mechanised cavalry units. Originally officers wore authorised piping in corps colours, while enlisted men wore unpiped caps; on 19 April 1940 all officers below general rank were ordered to wear intermixed black and gold campaign hat cords and overseas cap piping, and enlisted men wore corps-coloured piping thereafter. Distinctive regimental insignia were to

be worn on the overseas cap, and on the centre of the 'shoulder loops' or epaulettes. This officer wears that of the 4th Engineers, with the shoulder patch of the 4th Infantry Division. Officers of the Corps of Engineers were unique in wearing special coat buttons—all others wore the standard button bearing the Arms of the United States. The left breast pocket badge is a 1st Army Corps area rifle team marksmanship award. A similar Army area badge was also awarded, with silver crossed rifles, and a background in branch of service colour to the lower bronze motif.

The 4th Infantry Division was to land in Normandy on D-Day, fighting inland to join up with the 82nd Airborne Division. It fought in the ETO throughout the remainder of the war, reaching Miesbach on the Isar River on 2 May 1945, when it ceased active fighting.

B4: Colonel, 2nd Cavalry Regiment, 2nd Cavalry Division; North Africa, 1944

The 2nd Cavalry Division had been inactivated on 15 July 1942, but was re-activated on 25 February 1944, with all black enlisted men. It was sent to

North Africa on 9 March 1944, and performed garrison duties until the end of the war.

The overseas cap also came in khaki cotton chino, edged in the same colours as the olive drab winter-weight wool cap. On 25 August 1942 officers were ordered to substitute, for the distinctive unit insignia previously worn, their rank insignia; enlisted men retained unit insignia. The ranking of a colonel was a silver eagle, always worn so as to face forward. It is repeated on the right collar point; branch insignia, here the cavalry's crossed sabres with the regimental number, is worn on the left. The 2nd Cavalry Division shoulder patch was first approved on 3 May 1928.

C1: First Sergeant, 28th Infantry Division; United States, 1942–43

This NCO on field exercises wears combat uniform which was to be typical of the European theatre. The M1 steel helmet, first authorised in November 1941, was usually worn with the chinstrap hooked up over the rear lip out of the wearer's way. The 1941 pattern wool knit cap or 'beanie', authorised on 14 August 1942, could be worn under the

The M1944 wool field jacket—'Ike jacket'—worn by a member of the 11th Airborne Div. in Japan shortly after the war. He wears the paratrooper's patch on the left side of his overseas cap; paratrooper's qualification 'wings' on the left breast, and a Distinguished Unit emblem on the right breast. The only change in practice visible on this immediately post-war uniform is the use by an enlisted man of two 'U.S.' discs and two arm-of-service insignia discs on upper and lower lapels respectively, instead of one of each on the upper points.

helmet, with its rear flap folded down over the ears in cold weather. The olive drab field jacket, of (theoretically) water-repellant and wind-resistant cotton cloth, was first authorised on 10 November 1941. Formation insignia were worn on the left upper sleeve in the form of embroidered patches; see inset for the 28th Inf. Div. patch. NCOs wore chevrons on both sleeves of the jacket. On 22 September 1942 the grade of first sergeant was raised to be equal to that of master sergeant, and a third 'rocker' was added to the chevrons. Weapons for this grade usually included an automatic pistol as well as a rifle or, later in the war, a carbine. The trousers worn with the field jacket were still the olive drab wool type of the everyday service uniform.

Pennsylvania's National Guard, the 28th Inf. Div., was to land in France on 22 July 1944. It was badly mauled in the Hürtgen Forest that winter; its last combat was the drive on the Ahr River on 6 March 1945.

C2: First Lieutenant, 8th Infantry Division; United States, 1942
The officer's overcoat was first authorised in 1926. The buttons were of bone. Ranking, here the single silver bar of first lieutenant, was worn on the shoulder straps, and the formation patch on the left upper sleeve. These trousers are of the light olive drab shade known as 'pinks'.

The 8th Inf. Div. was to land on Utah Beach, Normandy, on 4 July 1944. It went on to fight throughout the NW Europe campaign, its final battles coming with the destruction of German forces in the Ruhr Pocket in mid-April 1945.

C3: Corporal, 1st Cavalry Division; United States, 1942
The coat worn here is the 1942 pattern mackinaw, first authorised on 26 November 1942; NCO chevrons and left shoulder formation patches were applied. The three-strap leather boots for mounted men replaced the laced type worn previously from mid-1940. The rifle is the recently-issued M1; as a mounted man this corporal also carries an automatic pistol, in the usual russet holster on the right hip, with two spare clips in the web pouch slipped over the rifle belt at front left. A first aid packet—the older, two-snap type left over from the First World War—is worn at left rear, and a canteen would be worn at right rear.

The 1st Cav. Div. arrived in Australia on 11 July 1943, and first saw combat in the landing on Los Negros Island on 29 February 1944. The division formed part of the invasion force which landed on Leyte on 20 October 1944, and fought in the Philippines until active operations there ended, officially on 1 July 1945.

D1: Sergeant, 45th Infantry Division; North Africa, 1943
The one-piece herringbone twill overalls were authorised for field use on 5 April 1941; they were supposed to be worn over another uniform, e.g. the khaki cotton chino shirt and trousers, but were usually worn by themselves, tucked into the web leggings. This NCO wears full marching equipment

with pack, including the large gasmask case worn under the left arm by straps round the waist and over the right shoulder; in practice this item rarely survived for long once soldiers reached the combat zone. The rifle is the M1 Garand. The divisional patch is worn on the left shoulder, and chevrons on both upper sleeves.

The 45th Inf. Div. was a National Guard formation drawn from the states of Colorado, New Mexico and Oklahoma; it landed in North Africa on 22 June 1943, and took part in the invasion of Sicily on 10 July 1943. The division was in the fourth assault wave at St. Maxime on the French Riviera during the US VI Corps landings of 15 August 1944; and saw its last fighting at Munich on 30 April 1945.

D2: Technician Fourth Grade, 51st Signal Corps; France, 1944

Although photographers were found on the tables of organisation of many types of unit, the Signal Corps was officially responsible for all the Army's photographic efforts. This photographer's overseas cap is therefore piped in Signal Corps orange and white, and he wears on it the distinctive insignia of his unit, the 51st Signal Corps. The overcoat was designed for both field and dress wear; it was not very popular in the field, however, as it became heavy when wet and muddy. The shoulder patch is that of 3rd Army, activated in August 1944, and commanded by Lt.Gen. George S. Patton Jr. during its famous dash across France and forcing of the Rhine. Commands smaller than a division and not assigned to a division normally wore the patch of the higher formation—that of their Corps or Army. The grades of technician third, fourth and fifth class were authorised on 4 September 1942; the chevrons were worn on both sleeves of the overcoat, although partly obscured here by the second-type photographer's brassard on the left arm.

D3: Brigadier-General, Services of Supply, 1942

The mission of the SOS was to provide services and supplies to meet the military requirements of all but the Army Air Forces, which obviously had unique requirements. As a full general officer this brigadier-general wears all-gold piping on his overseas cap. A single silver star marks his rank, and is worn on the cap, the shoulders of his model A2 Army Air Force

This private first class wears the China-Burma-India shoulder patch, and ribbons for the Pacific Theatre of Operations and good conduct. The diamond-shaped light olive insignia bearing a yellow eagle within a circle on the right breast indicates that this man has been discharged, but can still legally wear his uniform for a short time. By 1944, with a vastly expanded army and men transferring frequently from one branch to another, overseas caps were issued without coloured piping for enlisted men.

leather crew jacket (a desirable item, acquired through the unauthorised channels for which SOS personnel were famous), and both points of the OD wool shirt collar—general officers wore only rank and not corps badges on the collar. Over the shirt he wears the olive drab knitted wool jacket intended for wear under the 1941 field jacket. The Services of Supply patch is sewn to the left shoulder of the crew jacket.

E: Private, US Cavalry; United States, 1942

Strange as it may seem, mounted cavalry did not die quickly. Even the sabre was not eliminated as an issued weapon until 1934; it was not until 9 March 1942 that the office of the Chief of Cavalry was

eliminated, and the 2nd Cavalry Division remained mounted until March 1944. Even as late as November 1944 some serious consideration was being given to using mounted cavalry against the Japanese.

This trooper wears the cotton herringbone twill fatigue combat uniform, over an OD shirt and riding breeches and the boots seen in more detail in Plate C3, with the steel helmet. Practicing the 'pistol charge', he holds his .45in automatic, its butt secured by a lanyard passing diagonally around his body from right armpit to left shoulder; the doubling was held in the desired place by a russet leather slide. He wears the webbing rifle belt and braces, with the long bayonet scabbarded diagonally behind his shoulder, attached to the right hand brace. The saddle is the Model 1928 McClellan, basically the same as used before the American Civil War of 1861–65, with Model 1940 wooden stirrups.

F1: Technician Third Grade, Tank Battalion, 102nd Infantry Division; France, 1944

The 102nd Inf. Div. arrived at Cherbourg on 23 September 1944, and first saw action on 26 October. After its final action of the war, the capture of Breitenfeld on 15 April 1945, the division reached the Elbe River before VE-Day. Armoured units were attached to each US infantry division, and this figure represents a crewman from the division's Sherman tank battalion.

Specialised clothing for armoured units began to appear in 1941 with the introduction of this waist-length, weatherproofed cotton tanker's jacket. With its blanket lining and knit wool cuffs, collar and waistband it was a comfortable and popular item, much sought-after by officers and men of other branches. Early versions had a large patch pocket on each side, and later patterns had vertical slash pockets. In the winter of 1943–44 heavy, padded overalls with a 'bib' front were introduced for armoured crews; later versions eliminated the 'bib' and were cut straight around the waist.

The leather tanker's helmet had a high-domed skull for protection against knocks inside the tank, pierced for ventilation; and flaps for earphones held in place by leather-covered flat springs and by snap-fastened elastic straps to the rear flap. Introduced in 1941, it replaced an earlier type in russet leather which had featured a large 'doughnut' pad all

Two views of the M1944 wool field jacket. The patch on the left shoulder indicates current service under 2nd Army, which was a training army based in the USA, and that on the right indicates past combat service in a unit coming under Pacific Theatre of Operations command. The combined parachute/glider 'wings' are worn on the left breast; the medal ribbon is for Pacific campaign service, and—invisible here—in fact bears two battle stars. The jacket is lined with olive green sateen, stamped with the owner's surname initial and the last four digits of his service number. The only label on this corporal's jacket indicates a 38in. chest and 'extra long' fitting—'XL'. Note the rear tightening tabs at the waist, and the generally high quality of manufacture. It is easy to see why GIs preferred to keep this as their walking-out jacket, smartening it up even further by replacing all possible buttons with concealed snap-fasteners, and sometimes purchasing special high-quality versions of embroidered insignia, etc.

round at brow level.

Overshoes came in several styles. Black rubber civilian types with metal snaps were widely used; another type had heavy leather uppers and rubber soles, and laced at the front.

Rank chevrons and the divisional patch are worn on the sleeves. Tank crews rarely wore more in the way of personal equipment than a pistol belt with holster, clip pouches and first aid packet: their other necessities were stowed in nooks and crannies of the tank, and all armoured crews have a horror of being snagged by equipment catching on one of the scores of projecting assemblies inside a tank while trying to escape in an emergency.

F2: Technician Fifth Grade, 94th Infantry Division; Germany, 1945

By the Geneva Convention medical personnel were non-combatants and should not have been targets. They wore regulation brassards, and marked their helmets—usually with red crosses on white discs, but in some units with the crosses simply outlined in white. These precautions did not prevent many medics from being shot, however, and the Germans claimed that they were not sufficiently visible. In the 94th Inf. Div. medics in combat adopted this large white over-vest with a prominent red cross.

Over his M1941 field jacket and OD wool trousers this medic, snatching a hasty meal, wears medical pouches slung from his shoulders on braces; his personal first aid packet would be worn at the front of the pistol belt, which often had two canteens slung behind the hips, so that water could be spared for wounded men. Under his helmet this soldier wears the M1944 hood, designed for attachment to the M1943 field jacket, even though it cannot be attached to his own M1941 jacket; such mixtures of uniform items were common in the field. His boots are the double-buckle type which appeared in the last year of the war, doing away with the need for webbing leggings—see also Plate H1.

The 94th Inf. Div. landed in France on 8 September 1944 and was sent into the line against

The front-line GI: heating up a snatched meal on a field cooker, this squad wear the M1941 field jacket and, over their OD wool trousers, the trousers of the greyish-green herringbone twill fatigue suit as improvised combat dress. Note that most have the web chinstrap of the helmet fixed above the rear lip of the shell, and a narrow leather chinstrap from the fibre liner fixed over the front lip. (US Army)

the German forces holed up in the Atlantic ports of Lorient and St. Nazaire. In January 1945 they were sent against the Siegfried Line, crossing the Saar in February and reaching the Rhine on 21 March. Their last action was during the reduction of the Ruhr Pocket in mid-April.

F3: Staff Sergeant, 17th Airborne Division; Belgium, 1944
Specialised equipment for airborne troops included the M1942 jump jacket and trousers, sometimes worn alone, sometimes over other combat clothing. This suit had extra-large pockets for equipment, and tie-tapes from the inside leg seams helped control these when they were swollen out with rations, ammunition, and all the other necessities carried on the drop. The cloth used for this suit tended toward a khaki shade; subsequent reinforcement of knees and elbows with cloth from other sources sometimes gave a strongly contrasting 'patchwork' effect. The russet 'Corcoran' jump boots laced all the way up the ankle and lower calf, and no gaiters were needed. The M1C helmet modification is worn here, with the chin cup hanging loose; a first aid packet was sometimes fixed to the camouflage netting, for quick access.

Insignia include an American flag patch worn on the upper right sleeve for quick identification in combat: their role put airborne troops at risk in sudden encounters with friendly troops. The 'AIRBORNE' flash above the divisional patch on the left shoulder was common to all airborne units, though some had white lettering and others yellow. Rank chevrons were worn in the normal manner.

The webbing pistol belt is worn here, in preference to the rifle belt: a more flexible mix of items could be attached to it, an important factor for paratroopers. This NCO is armed with the M1A1 folding-stock carbine; its double clip pouch is slipped over the belt at front left. A first aid packet is worn at front right, a canteen at right rear, and an entrenching tool at left rear; the bayonet, or any one of a number of patterns of knife, was often worn strapped to the leg, as here.

The 17th Airborne Div. was activated on 15 April 1943. It served in the defence of the Meuse River line on 25 December 1944 during the Ardennes campaign. The division was dropped into Westphalia on 24 March 1945 as part of Operation 'Varsity', the crossing of the Rhine. Its last combat was on 18 April 1945 in the Ruhr Pocket.

G1: Private First Class, Alamo Scouts, US 6th Army; Pacific theatre, 1944
The Alamo Scouts were organised by 6th Army headquarters in late 1943, and trained to penetrate deep into Japanese-held territory. Their first action was a reconnaissance of Los Negros Island on 27–28 February 1944. They later formed part of a force which freed 516 Allied prisoners of war from Cabanatuan prison camp, 25 miles behind enemy lines on the Philippines.

Their dress was basically the same as that worn by all combat soldiers in the Pacific: two-piece herringbone twill utility fatigues. No rank or unit badges were worn in the field. Web gaiters were often worn under the rolled trousers, to discourage insects. Although most combat units in the PTO wore helmets, the Scouts found the twill utility cap—here in khaki chino—better suited to their type of mission. Identity discs—'dog tags'—were usually wrapped with black tape to prevent noise and reflection.

This soldier's weapon is the Thompson submachine gun. In a jungle encounter the first few seconds can be vital, and for the sake of initial firepower the 50-round drum magazine is fitted here; for later reloading box magazines are carried in a five-pocket pouch on the left hip of the pistol belt. A .45in pistol, pistol clip pouches, first aid packet, and two canteens are also carried.

G2: Second Lieutenant, 81st Infantry Division; Pacific theatre, 1944
The two-piece herringbone twill fatigues are worn with rolled sleeves, and trouser legs hanging loose over the boots. Photos in the divisional history show a camouflage pattern on the helmets, apparently painted to individual taste. Medical personnel also had very narrow red crosses painted on the sides of their helmets. Other than this, no insignia of any kind were worn: Japanese snipers were rightly feared, and officers and NCOs were priority targets. Minimal equipment is worn; the fighting tended to be of great intensity but covering limited areas, and agility and energy in the strength-sapping heat was of more importance than carrying unnecessary kit. The pistol belt is worn without braces, and supports only a canteen, a first aid packet, and a double clip

pouch for the M1 carbine—which has a second pouch attached to the butt. Most men seem to have worn watches. Out of the line, white T-shirts and herringbone twill fatigue caps were the usual dress.

The 81st Inf. Div. served in Hawaii until July 1944, but entered combat in the invasion of Anguar Island in the Palau Group on 17 September of that year. The division's 321st Inf. Regt. was moved in to relieve elements of the 1st Marine Division during the bloody fighting on nearby Peleliu on 23 September. Between 4 November 1944 and 1 January 1945 the 81st Inf. Div. captured Pulo Anna Island, Kyangel Atoll, and Fais Island. The division's last actions were fought during the mopping-up of Leyte, ending on 12 August 1945.

G3: Private, 17th Armored Engineer Battalion, 2nd Armored Division; Normandy, 1944

For the sake of visual logic we place this figure with two Pacific subjects; but he in fact represents one of the few US Army units to be issued with camouflage-printed clothing in the European theatre.

The US Army did much work in developing camouflaged uniforms, and an early type issued to some units in the Pacific in 1942 was of this pattern but made in one piece, supported by a system of internal braces. It was not a success, its one-piece design being highly unsuitable for men fighting in a climate where digestive disorders were frequent. This two-piece suit, which had a similar design in shades of brown and tan on the inside for use on beaches, lasted slightly longer; but the Marines complained that they in fact made the wearer even more visible when he was moving, and they were withdrawn in favour of the plain olive drab fatigues.

The 2nd Armd.Div. landed in Sicily on 10 July 1943, fighting there until November. They landed over Omaha Beach, Normandy, between 11 and 14 June 1944; fought right across France, the Ardennes, and Germany; and reached the Elbe River on 10 April 1945. During the fighting in the densely-wooded Normandy *bocage* country this engineer battalion was issued with the camouflage uniform shown here; it was as unpopular in the ETO as it had been in the Pacific, having the added disadvantage of similarity to the clothing worn by Waffen-SS troops in that campaign. The personal equipment of this GI, shown loading his M1

The front-line GI: a BAR-man of the 29th Inf.Div. photographed in the ruins of Julich, Germany, in February 1945. He wears the M1941 field jacket with M1943 field trousers, giving a colour contrast, and appears to have 'liberated' paratrooper jump boots. Note BAR magazine pouch belt; and the small-mesh helmet camouflage net, giving an oddly German outline to the helmet when held down by a rubber band—a rarely seen feature in 1941–45. (US Army)

Garand, is otherwise conventional.

H1: Technician Fifth Grade, Military Police, III Corps; Germany, 1945

This Model 1943 field jacket and matching trousers were adopted in response to complaints about the poor quality of the M1941 jacket. Of wind-resistant and water-repellant cotton cloth, it was in an olive drab shade generally of a stronger green than the M1941 jacket. First issued in 1943 to troops of the 3rd Inf. Div. in Italy, it was increasingly available in NW Europe during the last year of the war, but it never entirely replaced the earlier items; both styles were seen together, sometimes mixed in the same man's kit, right up to VE-Day.

Some soldiers went to the trouble of having extra cargo pockets sewn to the outside thighs of these trousers. The GI generally preferred to carry the necessities of campaign life stuffed into pockets and bandoliers, and slung from his belt, rather than carrying packs or pouches.

In 1944 a new combat boot, with built-in leather gaiters fastened by two buckled flaps, replaced the old ankle-length boot and webbing gaiter. The web leggings, with their many loops and hooks and eyelets, were hard to get off in an emergency, and the laces tended to break easily in daily use.

This military policeman is assigned to the MP company of III Corps, as shown by the triangular left shoulder patch representing a caltrop, an ancient anti-cavalry device. The brassard was regulation for all MPs, while the helmet was sometimes marked as illustrated, sometimes only with the letters 'MP', and sometimes left plain; in rear areas helmets were painted all white. High-visibility markings were important, since a primary duty was traffic direction near the front, often under fire.

The web pistol belt and braces support a .45 automatic in the usual russet holster, pistol clip pouches, first aid packet, canteen, and—obscured here—a carbine bayonet on the left hip. Carbine clip pouches are attached to the butt of the weapon.

H2: First Sergeant, 1st Special Service Force; ETO, 1944
The last Special Service Force was an outfit unique in the US Army. Including both Canadians and Americans, it was organised for Project 'Plough', a plan to raid enemy plants in Norway or Italy in winter 1943, to keep the Germans on their toes and guessing about the actual target of the Allies' forthcoming invasion. The 1st SSF participated in the airborne assault on Kiska, Alaska. After transferring to the ETO they fought in the Naples–Foggia and Rome–Arno areas before taking part in the landings in the South of France. The unit was de-activated on 5 December 1944, Canadians returning to their own army and Americans going into other airborne and infantry units. This young NCO wears the typical airborne-trained soldier's uniform, including the proud distinction of tucking the dress trousers of the OD wool uniform into jump boots.

The 1st SSF was an American Indian-oriented outfit, and the men were called 'Braves'. The left shoulder patch was a red arrowhead bearing 'USA' and 'CANADA' in white. The collar badge was a pair of crossed arrows, an insignia copied from the recently de-activated US Army Indian Scouts. The unit was distinguished by having its own coloured piping in red, white and blue, worn here on the overseas cap (which, like the rest of the uniform, was of US rather than Canadian design for the whole unit). The same colours are displayed in a lanyard round the left shoulder.

The cap bears the round patch in light and dark blue and white identifying glider-trained paratroop infantry. Both American and Canadian parachute wings are worn on the left breast, the former with a single star indicating a combat jump. He also wears the silver and sky-blue Combat Infantryman's Badge, indicating service in an infantry unit in combat. His medal ribbons are, from left: Good Conduct, American Campaign, and Pacific Campaign. The Good Conduct Medal required an unblemished three-year record.

H3: Captain, 32nd Armor, 3rd Armored Division; Germany, 1945
This battalion medical officer wears the M1944 wool field jacket—the 'Ike jacket'—first suggested by Gen. Eisenhower in May 1943 as a garment for both combat and dress use, like the British battledress. In practice the jacket was largely reserved for dress use.

This captain, in parade dress, wears the liner of his helmet without the steel shell, with his rank bars attached to the front. His scarf is in the maroon colour of the Medical Corps; such scarfs were worn for parades, off duty, and on duty in some headquarters. His 'Ike jacket' and wool slacks are in a matched shade of olive drab—in this case, the very dark, rather green shade found in many surviving examples of privately tailored officers' uniforms.

On the upper left sleeve is the divisional patch, in the universal design worn by all armoured divisions, differenced only by the black number. On each shoulder strap are his rank bars and the 32nd Armor's distinctive regimental insignia, pinned through the green cloth loop awarded to combat leaders. (Although medical men were not technically combat officers, this man wears the loop because he leads a platoon within an armoured unit—according to regulations this gives him the technical right to it.) This distinction was first awarded in the ETO during 1944. Note that this officer also wears, on his upper right sleeve, the shoulder patch of the 29th Inf. Div., a National Guard formation from the Pennsylvania–Maryland border country. The wearing of a second patch on the right arm indicates previous service in combat with that formation.

On his lapels are the officer's cut-out national cyphers, and the Medical Corps insignia. Above his right breast pocket is the gold-bordered blue ribbon of the Distinguished Unit Citation, awarded to the 32nd Armor for operations in NW Europe. On the left breast is the Medical Badge, awarded to personnel who served in a medical detachment with an infantry regiment or battalion in combat; he obviously earned this badge, analogous to the Combat Infantryman's Badge, when serving in the 29th Inf. Div. at an earlier date. Below the badge are the ribbons of, from left to right: the Bronze Star, with 'V' for valour; the Army Commendation Medal; and the Purple Heart.

On his right forearm is the golden wreath of the Meritorious Unit Commendation, awarded to units for outstanding services for at least six months in action after 1 January 1944. Above this are three bars representing one and a half years' overseas service.

The 3rd Armd. Div. was first blooded on 29 June 1944 in Normandy. Driving through France, the division reached Liège, which fell on 9 September. They broke through the Siegfried Line on 12 September; held Houffalize, Belgium, during the enemy's 'Bulge' offensive; and saw their last combat in the capture of Dessau on 21–23 April 1945.

For further reading

Britton, Jack, and Washington, George, Jr., *U.S. Military Shoulder Patches of the United States Armed Forces*, Tulsa, Oklahoma, 1978
Mahon, John K., and Danysh, Romana, *Infantry*,
Washington, D.C., U.S. Government Printing Office, 1972
Rosignoli, Guido, *Army Badges and Insignia of World War Two*, London, 1972, Vol. 1.
Steffen, Randy, *The Horse Soldier, 1776–1943*, Norman, Oklahoma, 1979, Vol. IV.
Stubbs, Mary Lee, and Conner, Stanley R., *Armor-Cavalry*, Washington, D.C., U.S. Government Printing Office, 1969
Weeks, John, *Infantry Weapons*, London, 1969
Sylvia, Steven W., and O'Donnell, Michael J., *World War II G.I.*, Orange, Virginia, 1982

The paratrooper carried a massive personal load during the jump, since resupply was so uncertain. Two comrades help this paratrooper secure backpack harness and equipment, before adding the chest reserve rig which can be seen at left foreground. Above the musette bag slung in front of his groin is a Thompson SMG with two box magazines taped along its length. The first aid packet is taped to the front of the helmet net, where it can be ripped off instantly if needed. Note (left) national flag patch, and holster for the folding-stock M1A1 carbine; and (right) leather shoulder holster for .45in. pistol. (US Army)

Notes sur les planches en couleur

A1 La ceinture a été remplacée en 1943 par un modèle en tissu cousu sur la tunique. La pièce rapportée sur l'épaule gauche identifie le service du grand quartier général, l'écusson du côté droit de la poitrine le service de l'état-major général. Les 'ailes' sont les insignes de pilote de ballon. **A2** La pièce rapportée sur l'épaule gauche identifie la division, les écussons en métal sur le bas des revers,

Farbtafeln

A1 Der Gürtel wurde 1943 durch ein an den Uniformrock genähtes Exemplar aus Stoff ersetzt. Das linke Schulterabzeichen bezeichnet die Zugehörigkeit zum Allgemeinen Hauptquartier, das Abzeichen auf der rechten Brustseite steht für den Generalstab. Die 'Flügel' sind die Qualifikation als Ballonpilot. **A2** Die Division wird durch das linke Schulterabzeichen markiert, das Regiment durch

placés sous les disques, portant les lettres 'US' et le numéro de régiment ainsi que les fusils croisés de l'infanterie identifient le régiment. La *fourragère* a été décernée à la 9ème infanterie en 1918. Le chevron sur l'avant-bras droit indique une blessure et celui sur l'avant-bras gauche six mois de service à l'étranger, tous les deux datant de la 1ère guerre mondiale. Le bloc de rayures sur l'avant-bras gauche indique des périodes de service plus tardives. **A3** La capote courte marquée seulement avec les barres de rang sur les bandes d'épaulette, la culotte et les bottes indiquent toutes qu'il s'agit d'un officier d'une arme montée.

B1 Uniforme typique de combat dans le Pacifique pendant les premiers mois de la guerre, alors qu'il était prévu que la chemise '*khaki chino*' et les pantalons serviraient d'uniforme quotidien et de combat en été. On utilise encore le vieux fusil Springfield et le casque de style britannique. **B2** La garniture de tête quotidienne aux USA était le '*campaign hat*', avec l'écusson du régiment porté sur l'avant et des cordes dans les couleurs de l'arme du service. **B3** Le '*overseas cap*' porté seulement par les troupes blindées et aéroportées depuis 1933 a été repris pour tous les rangs comme alternative plus commode que le '*campaign hat*', en matériaux d'été et d'hiver. A cette époque on y portrait les écussons de régiment: noter le liseré or et noir du calot d'officier. **B4** A partir du mois d'août 1942, les insignes d'unité ont été remplacés par les insignes de rang sur les '*overseas cap*' d'officier. Les lettres 'US' portées à droite sur la chemise par les troupes ont été remplacées par les insignes de rang pour les officiers; ils étaient de forme découpée, comme les lettres 'U.S.' des officiers, les insignes de l'arme de service et le chiffre afin de contraster avec les disques portées par les troupes.

C1 L'apparence typique du 'GI' européen commence à se profiler ici avec le casque M1, la veste de campagne M1941 et les pantalons de laine avec des longes jambières de toile. Le fusil est encore un Springfield; en tant que sous-officier supérieur il porte aussi un pistolet 45. **C2** La capote de l'officier a des boutons d'os. Ces pantalons sont les '*pinks*' autorisés en alternative à ceux vert olive foncé portés par la figure A1. **C3** Le *mackinaw* M1942, les bottes d'équitation à sangles de 1940 et l'équipement personnel complet, y compris le nouveau fusil M1 Garand et un pistolet 45.

D1 La combinaison de coton *HBT (herringbone twill)* a été autorisée comme uniforme de combat et était portée pendant une courte période en Tunisie. Il porte l'équipement complet de marche, avec le paquetage, et le large sac du masque à gaz en bandoulière sous le bras gauche; ce sac était en général abandonné rapidement. **D2** La pièce rapportée sur l'épaule est celle du 51ème Corps des Transmissions et le lieseré orange et blanc des Corps de Transmissions apparaît sur l'*overseas cap*. **D3** Un général des services d'approvisionnement pouvait obtenir tout ce qu'il voulait – y compris même une veste de pilote en cuir! Les généraux portaient leur étoile de rang sur le calot à liseré doré, sur les épaulettes de la veste et sur les pointes du col de chemise. Le pullover de laine est celui qui fut distribué pour être porté sous la veste de campagne M1941.

E1 La dernière unité de cavalerie n'a pas abandonné ses chevaux avant le début de l'année 1944. Cet homme de troupe porte la combinaison *HBT* de coton comme habit de travail, sur sa chemise, culotte et bottes. Le tire-feu du pistolet passe tout autour du corps en diagonale.

F1 Homme d'équipage du bataillon de chars Sherman attaché à une division d'infanterie. Le casque de char, avec écouteurs intégrés, etc., a été distribué à partir de 1941, ainsi que la '*tanker's jacket*' confortable et désirable avec ses poignets et son col tricotés. Les pantalons de protection rembourrés avaient initialement une bavette devant. On a utilisé plusieurs types de couvre-chaussures pour l'hiver, en cuir ou en caoutchouc. **F2** La capuche de la veste de campagne M1943 portée avec la veste M1941 – un mélange typique. Noter les nouvelles bottes à agrafes portées sans guêtres. **F3** Uniforme spécial de parachutiste avec poches extra larges, bandes de casque supplémentaires, etc. La couleur de l'uniforme était plutôt brun couleur sable que vert olive. On préférait la ceinture pour pistolet à celle pour fusil – on pouvait y suspendre un choix d'équipement plus flexible.

G1 On portait normalement des uniformes de corvée simples, composés de deux pièces, au combat dans le Pacifique; ce membre d'une unité de scout a préféré une casquette de corvée au casque. Il n'y a pas d'insigne. La mitraillette Thompson est équipée d'un magasin circulaire à 50 coups et des magasins supplémentaires 'boites' à 30 cartouches sont portés à la ceinture. **G2** On ne portait pas d'insigne de rang ou d'unité normalement dans la jungle. Cette division a peint des camouflages peu courants sur ses casques. Seul l'équipement le plus léger est porté; l'arme utilisée est la carabine M1, avec magasins supplémentaires dans les poches sur la crosse. **G3** En fait cette personne a combattu en Normandie, cependant le camouflage imprimé sur l'uniforme était plus commun dans le Pacifique. Il n'a pas eu beaucoup de succès.

H1 La veste de campagne M1943 et les pantalons assortis sont portés avec les bottes à agrafes de 1944. La pièce rapportée sur la manche gauche est celle du IIIè Corps. **H2** Cette unité de *paracommando* américo/canadienne porte des insignes spéciaux y compris les flèches en croix sur le col, et la pièce repportée d'épaule en pointe de flèche; une fourragère tricolore; et les "ailes" de parachutiste des deux nations. **H3** Cet uniforme de parade comprend la doublure de casque portée sans le timbre d'acier; on peut voir aussi la veste de laine de campagne M1944, '*Ike jacket*', avec de nombreux insignes – la pièce rapportée sur l'épaule gauche de la *3rd Armored Division*; la pièce rapportée sur l'épaule droite de son unité d'origine, la *29th Inf. Div.*; sur les bandes d'épaulette, l'écusson de régiment de la *32nd Armor*, ainsi que les barres de rang de capitaine, sur les boucles en tissu vert de commandant d'unité de combat; sur le côté gauche de la poitrine l'écusson de personnel médical qui a été au combat avec une unité d'infanterie; su le côté droit de la poitrine la '*Distinguished Unit Citation*'; sur le col les chiffres nationaux au-dessus de l'insigne de Corps Médical; sur l'avant-bras la couronne de '*Meritorious Unit Citation*', et trois barres indiquant 18 mois de service àl'étranger.

Metallabzeichen unten auf dem Aufschlag unter dem 'US' Zeichen mit der Regiment-Nummer, sowie durch die gekreuzten Gewehre der Infanterie. Die '*fourragère*' wurde 1918 der 9.Infanterie verliehen. Der Winkel auf dem rechten Unterarm signalisiert eine Wunde, der auf dem linken Arm steht für sechs Monate langen Einsatz in Übersee, beide während des Ersten Weltkriegs. Die Streifenblöcke auf dem linken Unterarm bezeichnen spätere Einsätze. **A3** Der kurze, nur mit Rangstreifen auf der Schulterschlaufe gekennzeichnete Mantel, die Kniehosen und die Stiefel identifizieren einen Offizier der berittenen Abteilung.

B1 Typische Kampfuniform für den pazifischen Raum in den ersten Kriegsmonaten, als die '*khaki chino*' Hemden und Hosen für täglichen Gebrauch und bei Einsätzen im Sommer gedacht waren. Das alte Springfield Gewehr und der Helm im britischen Stil werden noch benutzt. **B2** Die tägliche Feld-Kopfbekleidung in den USA war der '*campaign hat*' mit dem Regimentsabzeichen auf der Vorderseite und Bändern mit den Farben der entsprechenden Abteilung. **B3** Die '*overseas cap*' war seit 1933 für bewaffnete und Luftlandetruppen reserviert und wurde für alle Ränge als Sommer- und Winterausrüstung als praktischere Alternative zum '*campaign hat*' wieder aufgenommen. Zu diesem Zeitpunkt wurden darauf wieder Regimentsabzeichen getragen, man beachte ausserdem den schwarz-goldenen Schnurbesatz bei Offizieren. **B4** Seit 1942 wurden auf den '*overseas caps*' der Offiziere Rangabzeichen anstelle der Einheitszeichen getragen. Auf dem Hemd wurde das von den gemeinen Soldaten rechts getragene 'U.S.' bei Offizieren ebenfalls durch Rangabzeichen ersetzt; diese hatten ebenso wie das 'U.S.' der Offiziere eine ausgeschnittene Form, im Gegensatz zu den runden Abzeichen der gemeinen Ränge.

C1 Der typische 'look' eines 'GI' in Europa deutet sich hier bereist mit M1 Helm, M1941 Feldjacke und Wollhosen mit langen Segeltuch-Beinen an. Das Gewehr ist noch immer eine Springfield; als leitender Unteroffizier hat dieser Soldat ausserdem eine 0,45 in Pistole. **C2** Der Mantel dieses Offiziers hat Hornknöpfe. Die Hosen sind die als Alternative zu der dunkel olivgrünen Farbe von Figur A1 getragenen '*pinks*'. **C3** M1942 '*mackinaw*', 1940 geschnürte Reitstiefel und vollständige persönliche Ausrüstung, darunter das neue Garand M1 Gewehr und eine 0,45 in Pistole.

D1 Der Overall aus *HBT ('herringbone twill')* Baumwolle wurde als Kampfuniform ausgegeben und für kurze Zeit in Tunesien getragen. Vollständige Marschausrüstung mit Tornister und grosser Tasche für die Gasmaske unter dem linken Arm; letztere wurden gewöhnlich schnell weggelassen. **D2** Das Schulterabzeichen gehört zum 51. Signal Corps; der orange-weisse Schnurbesatz des Signal Corps erscheint ausserdem auf der '*overseas cap*'. **D3** Ein Offizier vom Versorgungsdienst konnte alles haben, was er wollte—darunter eine lederne Pilotenjacke! Generäle trugen ihren Rangstern auf der Mütze mit goldenem Schnurbesatz, auf den Schultern der Jacke und an den Spitzen des Hemdkragens. Der wollene Pullover wurde unter der M1941 Feldjacke getragen.

E Die letzte Kavallerieeinheit gab erst im Frühjahr 1944 ihre Pferde auf. Dieser Soldat trägt den *HBT* Baumwolle Overall als Arbeitskleidung mit Oberhemd, Kniehose und Stiefeln. Der Pistolengürtel wird diagonal um den Körper getragen.

F1 Besatzungsmitglieder des an eine Infanterieabteilung angeschlossenen Sherman Panzerbataillons. Der Panzerhelm (mit eingebautem Kopfhörer u.a.) wurde seit 1941 ausgegeben, ebenso wie die bequeme und sehr beliebte '*tanker's jacket*' mit gestrickten Manschetten und Kragen. Die gefütterten Überhosen hatten ursprünglich einen Latz. Mehrere verschiedene Gummi- oder Lederstiefel wurden im Winter übergezogen. **F2** Die Kapuze für die M1943 Feldjacke, getragen mit der M1941 Jacke—eine typische Kombination. Man beachte die ohne Gamaschen getragenen geschnallten Stiefel. **F3** Spezielle Fallschirmspringer-uniform mit besonders grossen Taschen, speziellen Helmschnüren usw. Die Uniformfarbe war eher sandbraun als olivgrün. Statt des Gewehrgürtel wurde ein Pistolengürtel gewählt, da man eine flexiblere Auswahl von Ausrüstungsgegenständen daran befestigen konnte.

G1 Einfache zweiteilige Arbeitsuniformen waren bei Einsätzen im pazifischen Raum üblich; dieses Mitglied einer Scout Einheit hat eine Arbeitsmütze anstelle eines Helms. Er trägt keine Abzeichen. Die Thompson Maschinenpistole hat ein rundes Magazin mit 50 Ladungen; zusätzliche Magazine mit 30 Schuss werden im Gürtel getragen. **G2** Im Dschungel wurden gewöhnlich keine Rang- oder Einheitsabzeichen getragen. Diese Division trug die Tarnmuster auf den Helmen, eine ungewöhnliche Einrichtung. Nur sehr leichte Ausrüstung wird getragen; die Waffe ist der M1 Karabiner mit zusätzlichen Magazinen in Beuteln am Gewehrkolben. **G3** Dieser Soldat kämpfte eigentlich in der Normandie, aber seine mit Tarnmuster bedruckte Uniform war im pazifischen Raum verbreitet. Sie war nicht erfolgreich.

H1 Die M1943 Feldjacke mit passenden Hosen wird mit den geschnallten 1944 Stiefeln getragen; das Abzeichen auf dem linken Ärmel bezeichnet das III. Corps. **H2** Diese amerikanisch-kanadische *Paracommando* Einheit trug spezielle Abzeichen, darunter die gekreuzten Pfeile auf dem Kragen und eine Pfeilspitze auf einem Schulterabzeichen, eine dreifarbige Kordel und die Fallschirmspringer-'Flügel' beider Nationen. **H3** Zu dieser Paradeunfiorm gehört das Helmfutter ohne die Stahlhaube sowie die wollene M1944 Feldjacke ('*Ike Jacket*') mit zahlreichen Abzeichen: linkes Schulterabzeichen der *3rd Armored Division*, rechtes Schulterabzeichen der ehemaligen Einheit (*29th Inf. Div.*), beide Schulterbänder, Regimentsabzeichen der *32nd Armor* und die Rangstreifen des Hauptmanns auf den grünen Stoffschleifen eines Kampfeinheitsbefehlshabers; auf der linken Brustseite das Abzeichen eines Angehörigen des medizinischen Stabs, der bei einer Infanterie- Einheit im Einsatz war; rechts die *Distinguished Unit Citation*; auf dem Kragen die Nationalfarben über dem Abzeichen des Medical Corps; auf dem Unterarm der Kranz der *Meritorious Unit Citation* und drie Streifen (für 18 Monate Dienst in Übersee).

WYLD

ISSUE 7 · WINTER 2022

IN THIS ISSUE:

Editorial

Mark Bilsborough

And so we make it into Year Two of Wyldblood Magazine – and what a great year it's going to be. Well, actually, with Covid 19 lingering like an unwanted guest who's outstayed their welcome, I suspect that this year is going to be anything *but* great, but it can't be worse than last year, right? And we have got some great stories to distract you (and very few have anything to do with pandemics).

Take this issue, for instance. We've got a welcome return for author Robert Bagnall, who gave us a fabulous cat in space Wyld Flash story called *Felis Sarcasticus* a while back and now returns with a bolts, rivets and dreams tale called *Inktomi and the Skyship*. We also welcome back James Rowland, this time with the unsettling *Cauldron of Metamorphoses*, plus tales of dark creatures, bright futures and poignant fantasy from Megan Sipos, Alison McBain, Russell Weisfield, Pricilla Santa Roas, Gary Gould, Rebecca Harrison and Chris Cornetto.

Moving into the future we're going to switch things around a bit at Wyldblood. This year, we're moving to a quarterly schedule to give ourselves time to catch up with ourselves. That means we should have time to do some other things, like novels (expect at least three originals this year) novellas and anthologies – we've got our steampunk extravaganza *Runs Like Clockwork* out in February. Then we'll be collecting the best of Wyldblood Year One and most of our wonderful Wyld Flash stories in a couple of bookshelf-friendly print collections – both out in the Summer. We'll also be commissioning stories for our next all-new anthology – *Other Earths* – very soon.

We are, sadly, going to have to increase our prices slightly. I hate price increases, but print costs, like everything else it seems, are rising, and we're still cheaper than most publications in this great writing community of ours. So starting with this issue, Wyldblood Magazine will cost a pound or a dollar more in most markets, but in return we're going to add pages and pack more in, like this issue's interview with top DAW author Jacey Bedford.

In light of our new schedule we're changing our subscription package too – so now you can sign up to four issues for £22 or $30 (approx) – a big saving on the individual price.

Another change this year will be the potential return of conventions, and we hope to see some of you there. We'll get you know on the website if we're likely to be at any events and we'll be sporting nauseatingly colourful t-shirts and probably talking loudly, so there's little chance you'll miss us. Eastercon in the UK runs from 15th – 18th April at the Radisson Hotel, Heathrow (London) so please pencil that one in – Mary Robinette Kowal and Phillip Reeve are guests of honour. Hopefully Worldcon in Chicago (Sept 1-5) will be happening too. It's been great keeping in touch with people over Zoom these past two years but that's no substitute for a well-stocked convention bar.

Our next issue will be out on April 13th and you'll be able to preorder through the website very soon. We're also stocked by Amazon (and many other places) which can be a good way to save on shipping outside the UK. Enjoy the stories,

Mark

Inktomi and the Skyship

Robert Bagnall

A shaft of early-morning desert light shone through the open hangar doors casting an incandescent stripe across the packed earth floor. It struck the naked framework of the skyship within, casting an angular shadow-pattern of lines and spaces behind it. The craft looked like a gargantuan insect, resting after it had wriggled free of its old, constricting skin.

Components destined to hang from the superstructure—bucket seats, propellers, control surfaces—sat at the craft's skidded feet. By them was a riveting machine, mechanical fingers that would blast each rivet flush, from which a long umbilical ran back to a silent and cold steam compressor sitting in the shadows where hangar morphed into workshop, tools hanging above benches on which sat vices and drills, lathes and grinders.

Alone in the hangar, Hoolian glared the steam compressor. It was a thing of deceptive beauty, at least to a man who had been raised with grease in his blood and smoke in his nostrils. Like a misassembled moonshine still, its main body was a squashed steel sphere, just too large to put your arms around, above which sat a monstrous, stretched horn going up and through the hangar roof. The outside of the horn was rough metal, but inside its surface was brilliantly polished, focusing the sunlight to an incandescent point where water would turn to steam. Upon and around the contraption snaked numerous pipes that led hither and thither; from the base rubber umbilicals sent the steam that powered the various tools. A regulator sat atop, its pair of heavy metal balls drooped, looking for all the world like disapproving eyes. To Hoolian it suggested an octopus, weighed-down with the sculpture of a madman who had a scrapyard and a forge at his disposal.

At some point in its past the name 'Endurance' had been stenciled on it, feather edged where the stencil sheet hadn't sat flush against the curve of the machine. Failing to live up to its baptism, it had wheezed its last the evening before, a seam or gasket giving up, perhaps a knock-on from some blockage, some localized build-up of pressure inside it. Losing power, he had pulled the cover over the suncatcher and Endurance had sighed and cooled.

If Hoolian could get into it, he knew he could diagnose and cure what ailed it. But to disassemble the compressor he would have to use the steam-wrench, which hung uselessly from the wall relying, as did all his powered tools, on the steam compressor itself.

Physician, heal thyself.

Quanto, of course, wouldn't take any of this for an excuse. And he had just a day and a half before Quanto would arrive for the proving trial. He just hoped he could think of a way to finish the machine without power.

Of course, he knew this was impossible. But his mind was a sea of competing voices: the naïve bluster of hope in the foreground, the clear-thinking logic of experience shouting against the wind in the distance. There was still time for him to sell his apprenticeship back to Quanto, to hand over the hangar, the half-built craft, his tools and everything else and walk away. Quanto would settle for that. *Quanto would be delighted to settle for that.* He could imagine the smile creeping across Quanto's insincere oleaginous face as he offered to 'draw up papers'.

A sixth sense pulled Hoolian from his reverie; a shadow passing, a change in the air. He turned and saw figures silhouetted in the gap between the hangar doors. Initially he assumed Quanto's flunkies had come to ascertain progress, before realizing these were strangers.

"Would you object if we came out of the sun?" A mannered voice, plummy vowels. Not a desert accent.

Squinting against the glare, Hoolian bade them enter. They shuffled inside, a strange pairing, the first short and squat, carrying a staff, wearing shapeless nondescript serge up to and including the wide-brimmed hat, albeit with a gaudy yellow waistcoat hanging loose underneath his jacket. He had heard no steam car, and everything about him, not just the staff, suggested he had not come on horseback. Indeed, suggested he had never ridden a horse in his life.

The second man wore a monk's dark brown habit but was somehow not a monk; perhaps it was the dark leather belt around his waist instead of one of rope. His head cowled, the slumped hood revealed little other than a salt and pepper beard on a jutting chin. Blind, he laid a hand on the guiding shoulder of the first as they moved into the shade of the hangar.

Hoolian bade them sit, gave them water. "I'm afraid it's tepid."

"Tepid is as cool as you can expect in the desert. My thanks," the traveler said, and for the first time Hoolian noticed his gloved right hand and bare left.

The blind man explored the edge of the bowl with his lips and they both drank in silence.

"I suspect that you should be busier than you are," the first ventured after a while. His companion, cloaked head down, continued to sip at his bowl.

Hoolian volunteered the tale of the steam compressor, how every powered tool he had depended on it, how it was the workshop's heart.

The traveler said sadly of the unfinished craft, "It reminds me of the skeleton of whale. Have you ever seen one?"

Hoolian shook his head, thinking *I've never ever seen the ocean.* "I am a master apprentice. I must build a skyship on my own to receive a release from my master. The various components—the mirrors, the boiler, the propeller—are all finished. It is just a matter of assembly. My wife will sew and dope the silk…"

"Is this why you have hidden yourself away here in the desert?"

Hoolian nodded.

"Who lays down these laws? Why not just employ a team? Many hands make light work. Let the machines you build proclaim your mastery."

"Quanto is my master. He lays down the law. He controls the mirrors."

The traveler considered, nodding slowly. "We have passed the mirrors on our travels. They are well guarded. They power the skyships?"

"The ground mirrors focus the sunlight, which is then aimed at the underside of the skyship, towards a ventral mirror," Hoolian indicated the circular cutouts in the framework, top and bottom, "which focuses it down further, boils water, and thus turns a propeller."

"And what if the wind pushes you beyond the range of the mirrors?"

"A dorsal mirror captures the sun and heats the boiler too. It's enough to ensure the craft can be brought back within the range of the ground mirrors. I started off as a mirror polisher. Aged ten. For five years I worked for a master skyship builder called Mancini. I looked up to him. Revered him. Then he said something that changed my mind about him."

The traveler looked up, interested.

"He meant it as a complement. He said, 'When somebody is excellent at something,

it is hard to imagine them ever doing anything else.' I knew at that moment, if I stayed working for him, I would never be anything other than a mirror polisher."

"A master mirror polisher," a woman's voice broke in.

The traveler looked up at the figure who had emerged from the shadows at the back of the hangar. The tiredness of her face matched the tiredness in her voice. He noted from the way her shapeless grey shift settled across her belly that she was heavy with child.

"But who wants to live and die as a mirror polisher?" Hoolian complained.

"Will you take some breakfast?" Ester said.

"Thank you for your hospitality, but no. In any case…" The traveler limply lifted his arm.

At Hoolian's blank expression he reached under his jacket with his left arm and, with a twist and a click, removed the offending limb and held it out, a metallic bird's nest of wires and rods and hinges.

"It's been in the wars," Hoolian said, taking in the buckling of its frame, the way it prevented rods from sliding, from fingers closing. He moved down to the wrist, observing how control wires disappeared into the traveler's glove. He lifted its edge only to discover, underneath, a real hand. Hoolian stole a glance at the traveler. A mechanical arm, but a real hand? What kind of magic was this? He knew better than to ask.

"It will take some work," he said uneasily. "Some parts."

"You cannot do it?"

"Oh, I can do it."

"But you need the parts?"

"I can fashion the parts. I just need a little time. Can you wait?"

"You have a skyship to assemble."

"The compressor…" He shrugged in resignation.

Whilst Hoolian worked, straightening rods, bending back an armature, sorting through springs, stamping a hole through a new metal plate, testing its fit, he spoke from the heart about the compressor's failure. Absorbed in his work, it was as if he was listening to someone else detail how his future—their futures—hung on a knife edge. With a working compressor he could complete the skyship, become a master builder, employ others. Without it, penury and destitution. Up to that point he had not dared admit, even to himself, how much hung on one machine, a machine that was almost certainly irreparable with the resources he had to hand. He scared himself with the truth. Vocalizing it only made it starker.

"There. It is fixed," he said, handing the arm back to the traveler who slid it back under his cloak, slotting it in place with a satisfying click.

"I surmise you would give anything to be able to complete your work," the traveler said.

Hoolian stared mournfully at the cold and lifeless compressor. "Of course I would…"

It happened in an instant. Like lightning or a mirror's glint. The traveler's companion, silent up to that point, put his hand on the shoulder of the first and the pair seemed to speak as one, a gruff growl coming from both and neither. "You will give what we ask for the chance to complete your project?"

Hoolian blinked and stared, uncomprehending. The pair repeated themselves. Hoolian's mouth outpaced his mind and, before he knew it, he had agreed to their terms.

"Then you will have what you ask and for this you will give your firstborn."

And then it was over—if it had ever happened at all. The blind man removed his hand, sat back and was again sipping his bowl of water.

"What? What did you say?"

But the traveler simply looked up in confusion, as if nothing had been said, as if Hoolian had imagined it all.

And when they finished their water, they took their leave. Moments later, Hoolian saw the steam compressor's pressure gauge twitch and the regulator shift. He had no recollection of winding the suncatcher's cover back.

Hoolian and Ester heard Quanto coming before they saw him. If anything, they smelt him before they heard him, an oily aftertaste on the breeze presaging the cyclical snort and blow of the steam car. Then puffs of white smoke from behind the ridge of the hill, in step with the breathing of the beast. Next, the open-topped car itself, stiff-backed chauffeur in goggles up front, Quanto behind on an over-stuffed leather bench seat, trying to give the impression of lounging whilst clinging by his fingertips.

"My chauffeur requires oil and water," Quanto said as he stepped from the car, brushing smuts from his linen suit.

For a moment Hoolian imagined these were the man's personal requirements before realizing his heavily pregnant wife was already hauling a zinc bucket to the handpump, narrowing her eyes at his immobility.

Quanto peeled white gloves from his hands, pulling each finger in turn, his disdain obvious, casting a sour stare over Hoolian's creation. He wore his mental processes as facial tics, his reaction going from disdain—virtually disgust, as if he had found something vile on his shoe—to resignation via uncertainty. "I suppose what matters is that it flies," he said, with a tone that foresaw anything but. "Krul will be your passenger."

An hour later, mirrors uncovered and steam whispering from the boiler, Hoolian felt the craft lighten and the skids move on the packed earth. Krul sat stiff-backed in the second seat. He had kept his chauffeur's goggles on but chose to hold his peaked cap in his lap.

And then, wobbling, they were airborne.

Easing all three valves, Hoolian sent power to the propellers, foot pedals holding the flaps slightly raised, guiding the craft upwards.

The skyship waded forward, uncertain. And then the props bit and the craft took a more definite step into the ether.

Hoolian glanced down. There was a definite drop now to the desert sand. The only sound was the woosh of propellers and the hiss of steam. He let out a manic laugh, turning to Krul. But the chauffeur could have been a mannequin for all the reaction he showed to Hoolian's joy.

More confident now, Hoolian adjusted the flaps to maintain altitude around hangar-height, sending power to favor the port side over the starboard. He would send the craft in a wide turn to starboard, followed by a port loop to come back to land where they had started. Perhaps ambitious, but it would be an incontrovertible demonstration of the craft's maneuverability. And given the air was still and the sky cloudless... he didn't want to have to start again another day.

Passing over Quanto and Ester he whooped and waved—neither waved back—before sending the skyship through a second slow loop in the opposite direction and, as planned, releasing hot air from the envelope and reversing the thrust of the propellers to settle the beast a mere fifty paces from where it had taken off.

An hour later Quanto departed, just as he had arrived, with the car disappearing over the brow first leaving a dissipating trail of steam in the sky above, whilst the gentle phutt-phutt-phutt took longest to be lost to hearing. He had left Hoolian with a memorandum of understanding for the supply of ten such craft, a line of credit, and a stamped metal disc. His mastership.

Such a small token, so dull and almost dirty, Hoolian's name stamped out in letters that didn't align. It seemed so pathetic now it was in his hand, this symbol he had fought for for so long. But it meant more than validation for his— their—efforts. It meant a future for them all.

Hoolian turned to Ester expecting to find her as joyous as he, as filled with victory. But instead she was bent double, slumped against the hangar wall, one hand to her belly the other against the whitewashed shuttering, her knees knocked from under her.

"It's coming," she said.

The baby was delivered on the hangar floor, amidst much screaming and cursing. At least Hoolian had hot water from the boiler of the skyship, but otherwise he was utterly unprepared, taking gasped instruction, female intuition, from Ester as the baby's head began to show.

Matters flowed faster than Hoolian could control or master, like trying to pause a waterfall with your fingers. But, like a waterfall, events took their natural unconstrained course and a minute later he found himself cutting the cord using a pair of tin snips.

"It's a boy," he said to Ester, holding out their son, so soft and wrinkled and pink in amongst the oil stains and swarf. She took him, held him to her, looking like Hoolian had only ever seen her once before, after she had fevered for three days and nights, lost to him, on the fourth morning turning her head towards him and croaking for water.

"He cooed. I thought they cried."

"He'll cry," she said, sounding strangely pleased at the prospect.

His face must have clouded as, when she looked up at him, her face as beaming as his had been when he held his master's tally in his hands, she asked quickly, "What's wrong?"

Looking down on the helpless infant there was a cold core to him. He remembered the words of the two strange travelers. He hadn't taken them seriously.

"Those two travelers," he began.

"Which two?"

He looked askance at her. "The one with the mechanical arm and his companion. I repaired it. You must remember. It was only yesterday…"

Bafflement. "The one with the arm, I remember. But he was alone."

Hoolian shook his head. "He had a companion. Hooded. I never saw his face. He sat next to the first and said nothing."

She searched his face, impatient for the laughter to burst, as if this was all a joke. But it didn't come.

"He sat in the shadows next to the first, sipped water from a bowl I'd tipped nails from."

She gave him a look, a look that said such a silly joke at a time like this was incomprehensible, that you ought to be ashamed, Jan-Carlin Hoolian.

"You were only here for an instant."

"I know what I saw," she said, defiant.

"The light, the shadows. It can play tricks. When I step out of the doors into the sunlight…"

"I know what I saw, and I only saw one man."

Their still unnamed baby threw a soft arm out to her, podgy maggot fingers pulling at her clothing. Ester exposed a shoulder, wriggled a nipple free, the baby latching on by instinct. As he suckled, Hoolian told Ester what he remembered:

the figures in silhouette, the irritation he may have inadvertently given them sanctuary from the sun for the day, the giddy moment when they seemed to speak in unison.

"You promised them our firstborn?" she asked, incredulous.

"I didn't offer. He just told me. He thought I would give anything to make the steam compressor work, and I agreed. And he said, for making the compressor work again he will take our firstborn."

Ester clutched at the baby, too tight, who, mewling and pushing, expressed his displeasure.

"I didn't offer. I didn't promise," Hoolian said. "He just said it would happen and he would take our firstborn. And it happened," he added sadly.

"Have you ever heard the legend of Inktomi?" she asked. "From where I come from it's something mothers tell their children about to stop them wandering too far. A bogey. A trickster. Wanting something for something."

"What's this got to do with…"

"He was always said to speak through a companion. A companion strangely injured…"

The mechanical arm, Hoolian thought. *The flesh and blood hand…*

"He would place a hand on his companion's shoulder and the words would come from deep within, as though the very ground were shaking the words into you."

At that moment they were disturbed by the distant hiss of steam, a scrape, a dull knock of something mechanical. Hoolian squinted to see beyond the hangar doors, but all he could see was the glare of the desert.

And then the distinctive woosh of a propeller turning over.

Thoughts tumbled: the skyship was out in the sun, its mirror exposed. The baby imminent, the sudden urgency, everything else had taken second place. The sun had moved. Less water in its tank meant it would boil quicker. "I've left the skyship powered," he said, running.

He had images of the skyship, uncontrolled, lurching into the ground, or turning to crash, unmanned, into the hangar.

As he reached the hangar doors, he saw the craft moving forward, its skids scraping. It lollopped upwards, came back down, bounced, and was airborne, its propellers beating out a bass rhythm.

Hoolian sprinted after it, expecting this fluke flight to end at any moment. But the skyship carried on level and true, travelling slightly faster than Hoolian could run, its altitude rising until it was beyond his reach, always just beyond his fingertips.

He could only run so far. On his knees in the gritty sand, sweat running down his back and his lungs straining, he looked up to see it execute a perfect, controlled turn, maintaining height at thirty feet or so and heading back in his direction. At the controls Hoolian was the traveler and, in the second seat, the hooded blind man.

His firstborn. They had taken his firstborn *skyship*.

A tumble of emotions that ended, inexplicably, given the fruits of a thousand hours' labor was being borne away, with relief. He laughed. Hardly the reaction of a man who was in the process of being robbed.

But not of his firstborn son. His firstborn *skyship*.

Rising and falling like flotsam on the sea, the skyship hauled its way against a gentle breeze towards him. He could see the traveler twisting the steam valves to equalize power between all three propellers, his feet twitching on the pedals to trim ailerons and rudder. And next to him, the pseudo-monk, his cowl pulled over his head, his robes wrapped around him.

Hoolian squinted. There was something on the blind man's lap, clutched within the robes. Something the man was holding tight to his belly.

Hoolian went cold. He collapsed onto the sand. His chest felt tight.

It couldn't be... How?

But as the skyship passed overhead, the only sound the slow beat of the propellers, he could see that it was true.

On his lap the blind man held a baby. His baby. His son.

The skyship maintained a steady course and altitude, heading towards the distant horizon.

He took the metal token on which his name was stamped out in skew-whiff letters and let it fall into the sand. For that he had, indeed, given his firstborn skyship *and his firstborn son.*

Robert Bagnall was born in Bedford, England, in 1970 and now lives in Devon, between Dartmoor and the English Channel. He is the author of the novel '2084 – the Meschera Bandwidth', and the anthology '24 0s & a 2', which collects two dozen of his fifty-odd published stories. He can be contacted via his blog at meschera.blogspot.com.

Vector

Gary Gould

The four of us are alone, sitting like the four points of a diamond inside the breachpod's cylindrical hull. We're strangers, but our names and bed numbers are printed on white plastic tags clipped onto our jumpsuits. There's an old man with thinning gray hair by the name of Lionel, a youth named Darrien, who looks barely old enough to be here, a woman named Wren, and myself. The breachpod vibrates at a level just below hearing. Fuel cycles and life support systems whir as we prepare to traverse the void between ships. There's no countdown. No speaker or headsets or communications. There's a hiss, a pop, a small jolt, and then I'm weightless for the first time in my life. We look around at each other in amazement.

My arms float above my head, and I notice how thin they are. I've been wasting away in bed for weeks as the orderlies cultivated the virus inside my body. I catch Wren's gaze. She looks as pale and thin as I do. Once, I could do the stairs from the

engineering deck to helm control twice in an hour, but now I can't take three steps without sucking wind. She giggles at being weightless. It's surreal. I realize that I've forgotten about the weightless void which has always been just outside *The Crescent*'s hull. We start to drift slowly away from *The Crescent*, waiting until we reach a safe distance to fire the rockets, then we will accelerate and change our vector to intercept *Farsight*'s course. With luck, we'll be one of the pods that reaches our target.

Darrien, the young man, sits on my right. A shaved head, hawk-like nose, and close-set eyes give him a sleek and predatory appearance. He looks around as if he's seeking a target and clears his throat.

"I want to see their faces," he says, "When we smash through their hull and run through *Farsight*'s corridors." A shiver runs through him and he closes his eyes. "We're fortunate to have this honor."

"Don't delude yourself." Lionel's voice is weak. He has a spotted head with white wisps of hair that cling to the sides of his head. "There's nothing fortunate in this."

"Do you know the probability?" Darrien says, "Of all those born on *The Crescent*, we had the right genetics that allowed for the grip to take hold in our bodies. And then we came into contact with the right strain of the virus before it changed again. We're here for a reason. I don't believe it's random."

"Fortunate or unfortunate, it doesn't matter." Lionel works his cracked lips around the words. He looks at me knowingly, arching his brow. *The youth are naive and arrogant*, the look seems to say, *they don't know true hardship*.

"If I could, I would rather it be someone else," I say. It seems like a cowardly thing to say, but now that we are out of the hanger bay and away from the crowd, there doesn't seem to be any point in appearing brave. "But it's us. We can't get out of it now."

The breachpod is quiet as everyone recedes into their own skulls with their own thoughts on the matter. Nothing seems real. The weightlessness is disorienting, dizzying, and it adds to the fever that's raging inside of me, turning me into a heat mirage one moment and a shivering sack of bones the next.

The virus – the grip is what we call it – doesn't affect everyone the same. Most people aboard *The Crescent* suffer a minor fever and body-aches, but every once in a while the virus mutates and meets just the right immune system to create an extreme infection. There was a time when we feared the grip and tried to destroy it. The captains of old tried to eradicate it. Whole swaths of *The Crescent* were quarantined, purged, pumped with radiation and exposed to vacuum. Generations of scientists tried to find miracle cures and vaccines that would wipe out the virus, but all that the research labs seemed to do was

suck power and resources away from *The Crescent*'s growing population and delay the inevitable outbreaks. *The Crescent* is an old ship, long departed from the moon where it was first constructed and started its journey. We've long been a poor ship with nothing much else besides the half-starved population that somehow manages to stave off killing each other. Compared to other ships, like *Farsight*, we have very little, but the current captain realized something about the virus which the others hadn't. We don't have to fight against the grip. We can use it. In fact, it's the most valuable weapon we have.

"I used to go to the machine shop everyday." Darrien starts to answer a question that no one asked. On his face is a fearful expression, and he's staring past Lionel, through the breachpod's hull, across empty space and back into the twisting corridors onboard *The Crescent*. "As soon as I was awake, before anything else I was there, asking for a chance to work. It was hard to get to the front of the crowd. Some of those people were sleeping in the corridor because they had nowhere else to go, and they were at the doors every shift to beg for a job. Once, I saw a woman breastfeeding her baby with one hand and reaching out towards a mechanic with the other, pleading that she would work the day for free, if only they would give her a chance. She was so skinny, almost withered away completely. It made me sick to look. But there was something worse."

"We don't want to hear this," I say. "You don't have to tell us this."

Lionel stares at the floor, which isn't really the floor anymore. It's impossible to tell which way is up. I'm sick to my stomach, wondering how much longer until we reach minimum safe distance and the rockets fire. Wren nods along, following Darrien's words. I shut my eyes, conjuring the face of my son, trying to see him in a happy place, like with a group of other boys playing tag in an abandoned hanger – anywhere else but begging at the feet of a crew member for a job.

"What was worse was I felt like I deserved it more. I remember thinking she couldn't possibly work – that she should go in a corner and die."

"Stop." I push against my harness, as if I could go over there and silence him in my present state. My boy won't have to witness such things. Not if we're successful. I know then that I'll do anything to see this through.

"The grip was with those people in that corridor," says Darrien, "That's where I must have gotten it."

"I don't know where I caught it." Wren's curly hair floats around her face. Her dimples belie her age, making her appear younger than she is. "I really don't."

Darrien keeps on: "Now I'm here, and who knows what happened to that woman."

"You say you're fortunate?" Lionel interrupts, "You don't know what's *fortunate* and what's not." Lionel spits the word as if it were an insult. Darrien doesn't seem to notice or care. He closes his eyes and tilts his head back.

My inner ear is spinning like a mad top. It takes almost all my concentration to keep from throwing up, but I've still got enough head-space to work over what Darrien said. What I don't want to admit is that part of me is relieved to be here. I won't have to fight to provide food for my family or worry about getting mugged by someone more desperate than me in the corridors. I won't have to watch my son enlist in the captain's crew and become a slave to the ship if it comes to that. I'm sorry I won't get to see him grow up, but I don't know how I could have lived through watching him suffer.

Wren looks at me, concerned. "You don't look so good, Asher."

"I'm feeling great," I say, tasting bile at the back of my throat, "A picture of health. How are you?"

She laughs, tinny and high. Her laugh devolves into a cough, and globs of mucus fly from her mouth and splash on the far wall. If I didn't spend the last few weeks in quarantine with all sorts of bodily fluids coming out of me, I might be disgusted.

"How much longer until we're clear?" Darrien asks.

No one knows the answer.

Our lives have been out of our hands since we entered into the Captain's service as vectors for the grip. We've stayed in medical wards, cut off from our families, and the orderlies have regimented everything we eat, every pill we swallow, always with the goal to keep us alive and keep the virus multiplying inside of us. I've had to push a button to ask for water, for the bathroom, for someone to come and help wipe the mucus off my face. The medical crew had almost two hundred vectors when they started, and at the date of our launch, there are ninety-eight. I feel a morbid sense of pride that my body is strong enough to handle the extremes to which the doctors pushed it. I don't know if this is fortunate, as Darrien believes, or unfortunate.

When we were in medical they gave us briefings about all the things that can go wrong with our mission. Our breachpod can miss *Farsight*. *Farsight* can have some sort of defensive weaponry that either destroys us or diverts us. Even if we successfully hit *Farsight*, we can be unresponsive to the drugs, or be too weak to walk. Then, there's no telling what's waiting for us on *Farsight's* decks. We can encounter a ready security team. We watched simulations showing *Farsight's* deck layouts and how to spread ourselves among the population as far and wide as possible because this is our ultimate goal. To infect the entire ship, we need to disperse as far as possible, leaving a trail of the virus in our wake. Then, all *The Crescent* has to do is swoop in and clean up the stragglers, and *Farsight* is ours.

The auto injector in my headrest whirs into place, answering Darrien's question: we've reached a minimum safe distance, and now it's time to hold on. The needle pinches my neck and the drug solution burns as it shoots into my veins. A few seconds later, the rockets fire. My chair swivels so the force of acceleration sits on top of my chest, pushing me down. I can barely breathe. My vision shrinks to a pinhole as the rockets roar. The acceleration is smooth, straight, uncompromising. The drugs kick in, a warm assurance that swallows up the panic inside me and turns the world fuzzy. As suddenly as it starts, the burn stops. The fuel tanks are empty. I'm weightless again.

We float.

Through the space between ships. The virus drifts through my blood. I see the analogy like a dream: our breachpod is the shell of a giant virus and we four are the little bits of replicating material inside. We four are strands of RNA, split off from *The Crescent*. And *The Crescent*, which is only one of the countless vessels of the flotilla that's spread across light years, is a living cell. *Farsight* is another cell. So is *Deep Wanderer*, *Ironshell*, *Warden*, *The Sol Stranded*, and many more – they are all cells in an amorphous swarm. Our vectors are veins, pulling us toward one another, pushing away, driving our mass deeper into space. We hurtle through stellar systems, looking for any place that holds more promise than the one we left. Worlds are just larger ships. Solar systems are just larger worlds. And galaxies are only the tiniest flakes of grit in an infinite universe.

I wait for the breachpod, my membrane, to make contact and push me into a healthy host. Warmth spreads down to my toes and my spine tingles. A hard knot of muscle in my back melts. I moan softly, floating towards my fate, feeling glad for my small part in the grand ballet.

The day I catch the grip, I go to the distribution deck. There's a mob of people in the corridor. Elbows prod me forward, and I trade turns stepping and being stepped on. I'm careful not trip on the sleeping figures against the walls. Sometimes the sight of the corridor sleepers makes me angry, and other times I'm afraid because I know that it could be me one day, but I don't feel sorry for them anymore. I separate out the part of me that would want to stop and help.

Crew members at the entry to the distribution center herd people in or out depending on the readout of a handheld scanner. A tall, well-built man stands among the crowd like a protruding river boulder. Men and women are shouting, trying to argue their case to the pillar of a man, who's face is a picture of bureaucratic indifference. I shove forward, heading for the gaps between shoulders and stretch out my wrist towards the man in the blue uniform. He catches my eye, waves the little scanner over my implanted tag. It beeps, then he helps to pull me out of the mass and through the large sliding door.

The distribution center is an old hanger bay cleared out and set up with red pylons that trace out the path of a long and meandering line. The path loops back on itself and runs along several tables where crew members are busy handing out rations, unloading crates, and running their little scanners over outstretched wrists to record each recipient as they take their allotment. It's a long wait until my turn comes, and I take the little baggies of dehydrated algae that are supposed to last me and my son for a dozen meals, but really only lasts half of that, then shuffle along in the opposite direction, winding my way back towards the door and the mad crush of the corridor. The man behind me is coughing hard and wet, like he's hacking up a wet rag. His face is pale, and he's out of breath. He bows slightly, apologizing for his condition, and presses the inside of his shirt to his mouth. Was it him? It could have been anyone. The next day I come down with a fever and as the days wear on, it only gets worse.

It takes thirty-two hours to intercept *Farsight*. I drift in and out of consciousness. When I can, I look at the other three with their arms suspended in the zero-g and their eyelids fluttering in REM sleep. I wonder what my son will be like at Darrien's age. Will he fall in love, or have a child of his own? Will he have my lanky build? Will he get sick, like me? Is there some sort of genetic tic or predisposition to the grip that's inside of me that he has also – something that he needs to worry about? I can see the shape of him, a spindly little boy who tries to run before his legs were ready and keeps falling but never cries about his scraped-up hands. His little mop of curly hair never stays tied back and in place. People tell me he looks like me, but I think he has a closer resemblance to his mother. He has a temper, like she does. I can feel him sitting on my lap. It's strange remembering the weight of him when the breachpod has no gravity. I reach into my pocket and draw out a picture of him, wondering who will find it on me later, and what they will think about the stowaway with a family who died abruptly on their ship. Whoever it is, they'll be dead shortly after. The grip has no sentimentality. It infects. It multiplies. It kills.

There's a port window in the ceiling, and suddenly *Farsight* appears, a huge spinning donut, three times the size of *The Crescent*. Pale starlight reflects off its hull and turns it a silvery color, looking like a moon with its middle punched out. It's silent and ominous as a grave. The auto-injector in my headrest clicks, and then the needle sinks in.

The cocktail runs cold through me, pushing out my warm stupor. My fever disappears, my head clears, and a giddiness spreads through my chest. I take a huge breath, flexing against the restraints. I haven't breathed so well in weeks. I can't keep a smile from my face. The others look around with wide, clear eyes. The pod shudders as it hits Farsight's hull. Gravity shifts as we enter *Farsight*'s gravitational field, and the chairs swivel to compensate. I undo my harness and find my feet, feeling like I could run forever. The hatch whirs and sizzles as the breachpod does its job, cutting through the hull and creating a temporary seal. The hatch blows, and Wren is first through. I follow close behind.

Suddenly I'm tangled up and can't move. Cold, slippery wires wrap around my chest and arms. I try to pull and tear them off, but that only gets me tangled worse.

"Hold on," whispers Wren. The light from the breachpod reflects in her green eyes as she works to free me. She puts a finger to her lips signaling quiet. "If we cut these lines, they'll find us quicker. They might not even know we're here yet. Come on."

She leads, I follow, and Darrien and Lionel trail us through the dark jungle of cables. Above, slits of light leak through and I can hear heavy thudding. Some of *Farsight's* security officers? Or residents? The gravity here is off, too bouncy. It smells acrid, and the air is thick, like I can chew on it. Suddenly I'm dizzy, saturated with too much oxygen. I put my hand on Wren's shoulder to steady myself. I half expect to see an alien walking towards us out of the gloom.

We find a ladder that leads up to a hatch in the ceiling. We pause to take a breath and look at each other one last time. Lionel is humming some three-note tune to himself on loop, and Darrien is tense and deathly silent. I feel a bond between us, born from our sudden arrival to this strange place and the danger waiting for us above. I put a hand on Darrien's shoulder and give it a squeeze.

"I do feel fortunate to be here with you three," I say.

"That's just the drugs talking." Lionel shoots me a crooked smile then returns to his humming. I decide the tune is something that a spacewalker sings to himself when his tether is broke and he's spinning out beyond rescue. It's some sort of shanty.

"Once we go through, we split," says Wren. We nod, and she starts up the ladder.

At the farewell ceremony, my son and his mother stand in the crowd with the other families. The hangar bay is cleared out and set up with a podium where the captain addresses the crowd. My son's forehead is scrunched up a way that's adult and solemn. He holds back tears and tries to spot me in the group of withered people on gurneys. I form my hand into a quivering thumbs-up. He won't see me cry. I'm determined that the last thing he'll remember of his father is that I was brave.

He sees my sign and looks away, blinking hard. I want to go to him, pick him up, tell him that it's okay to cry. He has been very brave so far, through all the time I stayed in medical. Each time I thought I would lose it and punch a fist through the plexiglass divider that kept us

separate, but I ended up smiling instead. He told me little jokes. He told me how he wanted to see me, but that he understood why he couldn't. My son, who barley knows how to write his own name, understands.

His mother clutches his hand as if he might fly out an airlock. Her lips are set in a hard line and her hair is tied back tight. Our history together isn't the best. Our son is one of the few good things that we've accomplished. We both love him. Despair leaks through her eyes. She's upset, barley hanging onto her emotions. She's not happy with this turn of events. Despite our falling out, she knows this is hard for our son. I'm sure she's sorry for me too, how could she not be? All of our fights and disagreements seem so insignificant now, almost as if they've happened to two other people I knew once. Catching the virus has eclipsed everything else.

The captain, a bent old man with a rusted voice, gives quite the speech.

"This is a fat, floating morsel," he says, meaning *Farsight*, "This ship is richer and more provisioned than I've ever seen – it can feed us for generations." He turns to look at us, his vectors, his feverish sacrifices. "This is for your children and your children's children. They will bathe in oxygen, and grow fat on bread and rice." I can tell by the look in the captain's eyes that he believes this, but there's also a cold, calculated gleam there. We are weapons: a means to an end. The *Farsight* and all its bounty will be ours when this is over, but that's not the end of it in his mind. There will be other uses for people like us in the future. When the captain speaks, I know he's starting a story at the beginning, and that the middle and the end will come even when I'm long gone. He speaks in verse and strategy, poetry and tactics – all twisted up together.

When the farewell ceremony in the hanger bay finishes, the orderlies come for us in their hazmat gear, divide us into groups, and push us through the airlocks into our respective breachpods. They move us efficiently and solemnly, like sailors following an order to load torpedo bays. My fever pounds in my ears and my head is heavy as I crane my neck to get one last look at my boy. Will he blame me for leaving? Will he forget about me? I imagine him visiting a memorial, a huge and cold metal plaque with my name on it, and lighting a candle. He nods once, doesn't shed a tear, and turns to continue on with the rest of his life. It's a fantasy, I know. Reality is never that neat.

I'm afraid. What if we fail our mission? What if *Farsight* repels us and all this is in vain? The orderlies finish strapping us in. They load the auto-injectors and pat us on the shoulders. We're heroes, they say.

Wren throws open the hatch and the light hurts my eyes. I scurry up after her, slipping on the metal rungs. At the top I crawl out on my hands and knees. The floor gives a little, like rubber. The air is filled with that acrid smell, and the colors are nauseating. Above me is a blinding blue ceiling and underneath my feet is a green carpet. My hands itch. They're covered in little bits of the carpet. It takes me a second to realize what it is – I've only ever seen it on recordings before – it's grass. *Farsight* grows its food in soil. The soil is the gagging smell. Some type of sun lamp beats down on the back of my neck. There are two and three-story structures spaced out between fields of crops. Irrigation systems spray arcs of water and long-armed, robotic harvesters work through the neat lines of plants. I recognize rows of tall, amber stalks: wheat. All four of us stand, dazed by the sight of it all.

Distant voices sound. Something about their cadence is frantic. Three figures appear from around the corner of a structure, holding curved, sleek looking pistols, or at least what seem like pistols to me.

"Run!" shouts Wren. Her voice snaps me out of my dazed state.

I make for the wheat, glancing over my shoulder. Darrien is off, heading towards a low field of cabbages and Lionel is blinking and looking up at the yellow ball of light in the sky. Wren goes straight at the trio holding guns. They shout to her in some language I can't recognize, then their pistols chirp and I see Wren's body jerk back.

Every bit of my training from the briefings vanish. My only thought is to run from the men with pistols, get as far away as possible, and don't look back. I plunge into the field of wheat, pumping my legs, lungs burning, hearing nothing but the swish of the tall stalks as they brush my face.

One of the structures is dead ahead. I exit the field, go up a small slope in the floor, and venture a look back towards Wren. One figure is kneeling next to her body, another is on top of Lionel, knee in his back, restraining the old man. Lionel is singing that lilting melody at the top of his lungs, off key, words garbled. The third figure chases Darrien's outline as he races up Farsight's curve, towards the line of the inverse horizon where metallic structures gleam. It takes a moment for my brain to decode what the shapes are. I'm looking down on the tops of buildings, and between the buildings are people – the tops of their heads – scurrying to and fro. It feels like I'm looking down from a great height and my stomach does a back flip. I turn away and head for the doorway which slides open automatically and lets me inside.

It looks like a family's quarters. There's a couch, some sort of digital display rigged into a table, and toys on the floor. A shiver runs through me as the drugs from the auto-injector begins to wear off. I take a few ragged breaths. The virus does a lap through my blood and hitches a ride on my exhalations, seeking out new hosts.

A little boy rounds the corner and comes to a dead stop, wide-eyed. My heart sinks. He looks just like my son. A second later his mother appears and places herself between me and the boy.

I stand dumbly.

She says something, but I don't understand her language.

I'm covered in grime from crawling through the bowls of *Farsight* and I haven't showered in days. The fever comes back with a vengeance, burning up my cheeks and chilling my bones. The mother's fear turns into something else, her expression softening but still vigilant. She motions to the couch right behind me. I sit, exhausted and shivering. The drugs are all burned up. Getting warm is the only thing that I can think of. And how much her boy looks like mine.

She follows my gaze.

"Mine's the same age," I say.

The woman shakes her head, unable to comprehend. I point at the little boy who is pressed against the wall, trying to disappear from shyness. She nods and says something, and the boy looks up at her expectantly. She speaks to him, commanding, and he sprints off. She looks back at me, scrunching her brows, considering this puzzle, wondering if she's doing the right thing with this stranger in her house.

"Mine would love it here," I say, forgetting she can't understand. This boy and my son could've been friends, I think. They could've played hide-and-go-seek in those fields. Mine would probably be afraid of all the plants because he's never seen anything like them before. The other boy would have to hold up the leaves and bend the stalks on each one so he could examine them. They would both be covered in dirt by the end of the day.

There's a tickle in my throat and then I'm hacking up mucus on the poor woman's floor.

"Mission complete, captain, just to your specifications." I mumble, "The grip is here. Are you satisfied?"

The mother shushes me, motions for me to lie down, and fills a cup of water from a spigot in the wall. They have water in their homes. Unlimited, clean, water. She sets it down next to me, but I can't bring myself to drink. Her expression changes to pity. I wonder how long her and her son will be able to fight off the virus before they die. It will take a few days for them to fall ill, but then it will move quickly. At the same time, other infections all over *Farsight* will be starting their course. Then the number of infections will double. *Farsight* will fight back. They'll have medicines and treatments and doctors with tired, desperate eyes, but it won't be enough. I know it won't be enough.

Gary Gould is a writer with roots along California's north, south, and central coast. He's published a few pieces here and there. His first published collection of short stories is titled A New Home and other short stories and is available through Amazon. Over the years, he has also edited many pieces for authors and storytellers in the speculative genre and beyond. Currently, he writes and publishes a new Flash Fiction piece every month at garyjgould.wordpress.com

The Girl who Cried Jewels
Rebecca Harrison

There is a king below the ground. He wears a tarnished crown. His robes are velvet and earth. If you pass a crevice, look down. That flash is his pickaxe. That spark is him striking the rock. That glint is diamonds falling. He toils for the granite men. He toils without end. No one has wept for him, not his kingdom, nor his wife. Once she cried until his coffers were full, until rubies poured from his turrets, until his moat was sapphires. How he smiled to see her tears. How he caught them in his hands. For each one was a jewel.

Now, walk three days until you reach a village in the crook of a river, and idle by the meanest home. More hut than cottage. Walls, more tumble than brick. Roof, more cobwebs than thatch. Step inside, breath the gloom. You may find a ruby stuck to your shoe. The poor folk who lived here craved treasure. Not the treasure of chests and maps. Nor the treasure of crowns and castles. They longed for the treasure of gurglings and chortles. A child. But none came. Days bended grey into nights. Silence held them. Tears lodged inside them. And so they prayed. They prayed to the bright folk who heave the stars, and the dark folk who dine on shadows. They wished upon the wind hogs that breeze over the river, and the snartlkif that lurks in the water weeds, fangs ready for dinner. They sang to the ghosts of silver mammoths and the spirits of fire bats. They even lit a candle to the granite men.

A child came. They named her Daisy. For she made a meadow of their days. When there were only scraps on their table, they feasted on her giggling. When there was ice on their windows, they basked in her babbling. The mother whispered thanks to the bright folk and the dark, the

18

wind hogs and the snartlkif, the silver mammoths and the fire bats. And the father lit a candle to the granite men.

One day, Daisy pricked her thumb on a thistle. She cried. But in place of tears, jewels sprang from her eyes. Rubies, sapphires, emeralds, and diamonds. The mother scooped them in her apron.

"Are we rich folk now?" she said as she tipped them onto their table.

"Thieving! You'll bring trouble to our door," the father said.

"Daisy wept them. They're her tears."

They left their hut, their tumble walls, their cobweb thatch. The mother carried Daisy across the village. The father carried the jewels. Their new home smelled of cloves and comfort. They lived among folk who didn't scrape, didn't hunger, didn't fret. The mother threw away Daisy's dresses that were more holes than wool. She brushed her hair and clothed her in silk until she made a sunrise of her. But soon, there were no jewels left.

"I won't go back to that wretched hut. It's only fit for blind spiders," the mother said. And she hugged Daisy tighter in the fire glow and silk shine and clove scent.

"Well, as I can see it, we don't have much choice. We've spent our last diamond," the father said. "Unless Daisy cries us another."

"I won't have her afeared." The mother stroked Daisy's golden hair.

"Will you have her poor?"

The mother paced the thin hours. Hours thin as the gruel she once ladelled into bowls. Hours thin as the blanket she once huddled beneath. Daisy was her treasure, her meadow, her sunrise. A pain bloomed in her heart.

"She need only cry once. Once would be plenty," she said to the oak shadows.

In the morning, Daisy toddled in the fields. The bluebells and winds teased her. The sky was fast with swallows. The day was as warm as a butterbear's belly, but the mother felt as chill as a silver mammoth's sleep.

"Just once," she said to the sparrows. And she pushed Daisy, made her fall, made her bruise. Daisy wept rubies and sapphires and emeralds and diamonds. The mother scooped them into a velvet purse.

"It's done." She dropped the purse by the father's boots. "Now she need never weep."

But the jewels were spent. And 'never' became 'again' became 'often' became 'always'.

Walk East until the Dog Star blinks ten times, and on the horizon, you'll spy a house grand as a sea goddess's palace. Count the windows. The twenty third was Daisy's. She sat here, her window flung open to rain, and she shared her scraps with the starlings. For that's what her mother and father fed her: scraps. They forgot she was their treasure, their meadow, their sunrise. She became their bank, their coffers, their jewel mine. Cruel words they spoke to her. Words of thistles and bruises. Words that pricked her eyes and made the jewels fall. And they made a hoar frost of their home.

Daisy grew up, her only friends starlings and jays, moonlight and wisps. She was a secret, a soft footstep, a swift shadow. And if a guest glimpsed her, the mother and father would tell them a tale. The golden ghost, they called her.

"Such a sorrowful story," the mother said, sipping from a silver goblet. "As bonny a girl as any you'd see. Hair like buttercups, skin pink as a bitten apple. But there was no joy in her. None. And she cried so much, she cried herself to nothing." And she glanced towards the curtain where Daisy hid. There were sapphires on the floorboards.

Daisy's belly always grumbled. Her heart was always sore. She sat by her window, moonshine puddling on her shining hair. There was a tap on the glass.

"Drackle!" She opened the window. A magpie hopped inside, his beak stuffed with copper leaves and hedgehog quills. He sat them at her feet and perched on her lap. She stroked his head. "A fair exchange," she said, unwrapping her handkerchief. He pecked at the pie crust. "Now we've dealt with trade, tell me of the woods, or the winds shaking the oaks, or the leaves bursting in a swirl," she said. "It's a dance, and I'm straining for the music, the piping soft as rain. Can you hear it, Drackle?" He tilted his head. "Help me sew. Then I shall know it for myself. I will wear leaves in my hair and join the winds' dance and sing with the piper." She unwrapped a garment. A green velvet cloak smelling of wine and cruelty. "It was my mother's. But she has so many, she won't notice. And she wouldn't know it now. See!" She held it up. On the other side, were quills, feathers, bracken, and leaves. "I will wear this and be hidden. And folk who do see me, shall think me a hedgemaiden and leave me snail shells." She threaded a needle and began to sew the copper leaves on to the cape. "I will never come back here." A ruby fell from her eye. "Take it, Drackle." She handed him the jewel.

He flew back to the woods, the gem glinting in his beak, but a savage wind tumbled him. He dropped the ruby. Down it fell, bumping against an oak trunk and landing in a heap of lichen. A sound rang through the woods, like a gasp if a gasp was rock. A granite man pulled the jewel from his lichen beard. He knew this ruby. He turned it in his grey fingers. He had watched it grow in the far down of the earth, where the rock meets forever, where the dark becomes jewels. Drackle landed

between bending oaks and ferreted in the leaf mulch for his gem. There was a sound like laughter if laughter was lava cooling to stone. He looked up, saw his ruby in the grey grip, flapped his way into the high bare branches, and watched the granite man's slow tread through the forest.

And so, Daisy sewed by star blink and moon smudge, her magpie all chatter and nudge. Each leaf an escape. Each quill a path. Each stitch a horizon. Her fingers ached but her heart uncurled. She fell asleep with Drackle in her arms. By day, the mother and father taunted gems from her, collecting them in teacups and buckets. Until, one night, Daisy threaded the last quill onto the cloak.

"It's finished, Drackle," she said. She wrapped the cloak around her shoulders. It smelled of peat and hiding places. "At dawn, they will find me gone. Do they know how they've hurt me, or do they only count my pain in jewels?" She cried sixteen diamonds, one for each of her years. "I won't weep for them again." She put her tears in her purse and tucked it under her cloak.

She whisper-stepped through the corridors, the archways, the spiralling towers. She stole a pie from the pantry. Drackle was a swift shape in the shadows. She followed him out into the winds. And then they were fast in fields and frost and fog.

"Can you see the horizon, Drackle?" Daisy whispered. He settled on her shoulder as the woods flung up around them. She pushed her hood down to let the winds into her hair. She breathed the night. The scent of lichen and rock. The sound of a granite head turning to watch. On she walked. She never heard her mother's shock. She didn't feel her father's rage. She didn't see their carriage race.

"Faster," the mother spat as the horses rattled through the day. By dusk, they reached the King's castle. The sun bowed below the turrets.

"His Highness owes us. If he doesn't help us, we'll demand our diamonds back. And how will he pay for his knights then? Or his ships? Or his wars?" the father said. They waited among the torch light and courtier whispers for the sound of the King's footsteps. The mother dropped into a curtsy. The King was handsomeness made cruel.

"Your Highness, our daughter has gone. She is all to us. We beg you to send your men to find her and bring her back to us," she said.

"Daughter? Why have you hidden her all these years?"

"She is a tender girl, too timid for the world of men," she said.

"And yet, you have lost her." The King gestured for her to rise.

"We need your help. And if we don't get her back, that's it, we won't have any more jewels for ourselves, let alone for you," the father said.

"And why's that?" the King said.

"My husband just means that Daisy is our treasure, your Highness."

So, the King sent his men to the forests.

"The jewels came from their daughter," he muttered to himself. "But how? And why has she fled?" And he paced hours guessing and waiting. But his men couldn't find Daisy. They were seeking a girl of silk and gleam, not a maid of quill and bracken. They rode past her.

She walked on. The pie was soon gone. Her belly was louder than crows. Her hands were numb. Dusk caught in the oaks. Sunset snipped the clouds. Snow fell. She curled in a hollow and tried not to ache. Drackle nested under her cloak. She closed her eyes. She didn't hear the footsteps.

"Well, hedge maid, you can't go sleeping out in this snow, not if you want to wake up with all your toes," said a voice like firewood. She opened her eyes. An old lady leaned on a cane. "Come with me or you'll be ice before midnight." Daisy scrambled to her feet. Drackle hopped out from under her cloak. The old lady nodded. "I'm Bessy."

"Daisy, and this is Drackle." They walked, heart deep in silence and snowfall. A hut leaned between the bare trees. Bessy led her into the smell of carrots baked sweet and crackling twigs.

"Hungry?" Bessy asked as she scooped carrot soup into a bowl. Daisy could only nod. She slurped one warm bowl and a second and a third. Bessy laughed. "You can sleep in the chair by the fire." And Daisy did. Embers cosied into her dreams. She woke before dawn. Bessy had left her a chunk of bread on the table. She nibbled it in the blue gloom, sharing crusts with Drackle.

"I must give her something. No one has ever been kind to me before," she said. Drackle flapped his wings. "No one but you." She opened her purse and took out a diamond. Then she crept out into the snow. She didn't see the granite figure by the wall, didn't see stone eyes blink, didn't hear a sound like a murmur if a murmur was marble. Then she was gone.

The granite man peered in the window. He knew that diamond. He had heard it form in the low places of the earth, where the stone leans into always, where the silence turns to gems. He watched Bessy gasp, grip the jewel, clutch it close. Then he moved through the bare oaks. Snow settled in the crags of his face. Frost lit his lichen beard. He walked into the barrows. The earth closed behind him. Darkness held him, coaxed him, led him. Into the deep places, he walked. Other voices met him, other shapes, other breath. Perhaps you have heard these voices, too? When the wood thickens, hold still. Listen below the

21

roots. The granite men don't speak of their missing jewels now. But they did when Daisy walked the woods. Their gems were vanishing. They blinked from the rocks. They had been disappearing since the day she pricked her thumb on a thistle, since she first wept. The granite man spoke of the hedgemaid and her diamond. And the granite men walked from the barrows. To listen. To watch. To follow.

Daisy went on through the woods. Poor folk shared their fires and their pies, their shelter and their laughter. She left them diamonds. And whispers of her blew through the woods, the villages, the fields, all the way to the castle.

"Where did a hedgemaid find diamonds?" the king said. And he thought of his coffers, his ships, his wars. "She's their daughter. They want her for her jewels. They must have been cruel." He saddled his horse and rode out with his men.

"I feel eyes following me, Drackle," Daisy said as they took a path between birches. Snow clogged the quills on her cape. Her breath was puffs. "But when I turn, there's no one there. Is it my fancy?" Drackle cawed and circled. Daisy looked round: snow sparked and trees hushed. The woods smelled of badgers and stone. "Mine are the only shoe prints." She wrapped her cloak tighter. "Come, Drackle." She took swift steps. The wind was still, but she heard branches bending. She felt the ground trembling. There was a sound like laughter if laughter was a white cliff crumbling. She froze. Drackle was in her arms. And then she was turning around. A man of stone was following her. His gaze met hers. She clutched Drackle harder. Stone men trekked from the deeps, branches snapping, trees bending. She ran. She couldn't feel her feet. Her breath was gasps and cries. She heard them faster behind her. She stumbled. Suddenly, a

horse was in front of her and a man was reaching for her. Hands pulled her onto the horse. She held on. He rode and rode. She felt Drackle on her cloak. She didn't look back.

"Where are we?" she asked as woods became fields became towers.

"My home, Hedgemaid. Don't you recognise me?" He halted the horse in front of the castle. She jumped down. "Don't flee. You're safe here. You may stay as long as you wish. Forever, if you choose." He held out his hand. "Or just for dinner." She glanced towards the wood, felt the tremor of stone steps following, and took his hand.

"I demand a place at the table for my magpie," she smiled.

"He shall be guest of honour," the king said.

Daisy took off her cloak. The hall was tapestry and torch light, spice and syrup. She dined until her belly ached from eating, talked until her jaw hurt from laughing. Drackle perched at the Head of the Table and pecked at a silver goblet. The king told tales of banners and beasts. She slept in a round room, soft with velvet, Drackle nesting on her pillow.

A clamour of words woke her. Words shouting in a hall. Words echoing up the tower. Her mother's words. Then a knock on her door.

"Your mother and father are here, Hedgemaid. One word from you, and I shall send them away," the king said. He stepped into her room. "Be my Queen."

"You want us to wed?" She was already wrapped in her cloak.

"There's never been a hedgemaid queen before. Will you be the first?" He reached out his hands to her. "Or will you go back with your mother and father?"

So they wed, though Daisy wore her quill cloak, though Drackle perched on her shoulder. The vows were strange shapes in her mouth. The torchlight flared like stinging flags. Courtiers watched all murmur and gawp. Music sharp and sweet held her as they danced.

"How do you make your jewels, Hedgemaid?" the King said into her ear.

"I never made them," she said as she danced.

"Tell me, or do I have to find out for myself?" And he took her in his arms. His face was handsomeness made with spite and winter.

"The jewels are my tears," she said.

"Cry for me."

"I cannot."

"Then I shall make you." And he took her from the hall, dragged her to his chambers, slammed Drackle out of the room. All night, through hours long with Daisy's cries, with the King laughing as he scooped handfuls of diamonds, Drackle scratched at the door. At dawn, the King let him in. The chambers were kneel deep in jewels.

The king paid his debts. Towers crammed with gems. Diamonds dripped from the turrets. Sapphires overflowed the moat. Rubies scattered over the fields. Emeralds tucked into horses hooves and were trod into far off roads. Roads that dwindled into paths. Paths that shrank to trails in the trees. Trees the granite men wandered between. And so they found and followed their jewels.

Daisy sat on her throne beside the king. There were rubies on her cheeks. Drackle perched on her shoulder. The castle smelled of sapphires and hurt.

"Hold your head up. Try to look like a queen," he said. She brushed the jewels from her face, scattering them across the hall. There was a trumpet and then a voice bellowing her parents' names. She jolted. And then they were before her.

"Your Highness," her mother said, curtseying low to the king. "As you know, you have our only child by your side. All we ask if that she be returned to us for one day a fortnight. One day when we can treasure her."

"Your daughter is my queen now. She has duties here."

"We miss her," the father said.

"You miss her jewels. I tire of this. You may collect as many jewels from her as you can before the clock strikes midnight."

"Thank you, Your Highness." And her parents moved towards her. Drackle cawed at them. He lunged for the mother's hands.

"It is time that bird was dealt with," the king said. He gestured to a guard. Daisy gripped Drackle and ducked out of her mother's reach.

"Leave him alone," she said. Suddenly, hands locked her arms, took Drackle from her. "Let him go," she screamed at the guards. She tried to shake free. The air wheeled. The ground began to tremor, began to shiver, began to shake. And she smelled granite and lichen. "The grey men." Stone steps thudded through the corridors. A crack etched up to the ceiling.

"Who goes there?" the King shouted. A window shattered. And then the granite men were in the hall. A grey hand pointed at Daisy. She felt the day twisting. Her breath was sharp in her throat. "Who are you?" the King said. Granite heads turned. Granite eyes fixed him. He quaked.

"We come for our jewels," they said in one voice. One voice that scratched the walls. Daisy felt caught and falling.

"The only jewels here are mine."

"We come for our jewels," they said. A granite man stepped forward. The king cowered behind his throne. The granite man snatched the throne and dashed it aside.

"She has them," the king pointed at Daisy.

"Don't," Daisy gasped.

"I didn't know they were yours. She cries them. They're her tears." The granite men turned to look at Daisy. "Tell them," he urged her parents.

"She's been weeping jewels since she was a tot," her mother said. "It's her, not us. We didn't know. It's always been her."

"Show them," the king commanded his guard. He let go of Daisy for a moment. Then he lifted a gloved hand and hit her across her face. Diamonds sprang from her eyes, clattering on the floor. A granite man knelt and lifted a jewel. "See. It's her. Take her. She's yours." Daisy felt stone eyes grazing her. Her heartbeat hurt.

"She cries the jewels," the granite man said. "She shall cry no more." Suddenly, the granite men were moving, were seizing the king and her mother and father, lifting them, and carrying them out and out. And then down and down, into the earth, into the dark. They still toil below the ground.

And there were no more tears in the kingdom. Not while Queen Daisy ruled, her magpies on her shoulders, her cloak of quills and bracken. She ruled for many years. Years mellow as bluebells shaking. Years soft as a dove's belly. She grew old and loved. There was always a smile in her voice, always a greeting in her hands, and always a crust for a bird. Until the day they found her in the deepest sleep of all, the sleep without dreaming, without waking. And tears returned to the kingdom. And the folk followed her coffin, their heads bowed and their hearts low. But the magpies led the procession, and they guard her grave now.

Rebecca Harrison sneezes like Donald Duck and her best friend is a dog who can count. She was chosen for the WoMentoring Project by Kirsty Logan and long listed for this year's Wigleaf's top fifty.

Asylum

Alison McBain

If he'd known when he killed her what would come of it, would he still have done it? Would he have condemned an entire race to die?

I'll never know. I didn't know him personally, you see. Just like everyone else, I saw him on TV. Everywhere, people were talking about him, speculating. He was the first Allam to be arrested for a crime such as this.

Don't think that we're different just because of our past. No, we're the same. I grew up surrounded by others born on American soil. I learned to put up the flag on the Fourth of July. I am a patriot as much as anyone can be.

But it ended there. Now, I am in a cage, along with everyone else who is first or second generation Allam. I'm second, in case you didn't understand from my rambling. Born here on Earth. I've never been anywhere else, so when the humans shout out for me to go back home, I want to yell back at them: "I am home, you morons. This is my home, as much as it is yours."

But I won't get the chance. They're gonna gas us. Or chop us. Or follow the advice of the mob and send us "home."

Mother looked frightened all the time after we heard about the murder. She guessed what was coming for us. And going home is as much a death sentence for her as it is for any other Allam. They might as well just kill us and save themselves the cost of the trip.

I keep hoping for a reprieve, but my mind goes around in circles. We had rights just like everyone else, once. How did it change so fast?

"Your name is *Sally*?"

And the class erupted into laughter.

"That's enough," said the teacher. Then, more sharply, "That's *enough*, class." The laughter began to fizzle, but every so often one of the children would let loose a snort. Mrs. Marks turned her razor-sharp glare on the boy who had spoken. "Jeffrey, please apologize to Sally."

"What did I say?" he asked.

"Jeffrey!" she said in that don't-argue-with-me tone of voice perfected by teachers and parents over the ages.

"I'm sorry," he muttered.

"Thank you, Jeffrey," answered a stilted, mechanical voice--my voice.

Even Mrs. Marks couldn't control the class after that.

I spent most of that day--and the next one and the one after that--at my desk, trying not to talk through my translator. Mrs. Marks called on me more than she should have, and hovered near my desk when she walked the aisles, but it just emphasized the difference between the other kids and me. When I got home, Mother asked the eternal question of parents: "How was your first day of school, dear?"

I sighed. "I don't see why you had to send me to public school. Why couldn't you let me go to the special school for us?"

Mother sighed. "I know you don't understand now, but someday--"

"May I please be excused?" I interrupted. She shrugged her tentacles, but let me go.

Eventually, I did make friends. There are always people who pride themselves on being immune to prejudice. I have found that it is a type of prejudice all by itself. When I was invited over to play, the parents tried too hard, and I felt as if my skin were crawling with ants, it was so uncomfortable trying to be nice to them.

"Oh, we love the Allams' contributions to America," said Helen's father. Helen and I were best friends, but her parents seemed awkward whenever I was around. He continued, "A co-worker of mine is good friends with an Allam."

It's a misnomer, though it has stuck in pop culture. I'm not an "Allam," an Alien American. No more than the Haudenosaunee were Indians from India. Our name isn't pronounceable in human languages, though. On our native world, my kind spend half our time in the ocean and half on land. Our language is only spoken in water, so there is no translation for it in the air.

There were only one thousand refugees on that first ship, the one my parents arrived on. They were among the first to be granted asylum in the U.S. Over the next five years, the Resistance sent two more ships here before something happened back home, and then the ships no longer came. We don't know what stopped them, but we can guess.

My parents don't talk about it at all. All this is information I found out from everyone except my parents--but they couldn't stop me from hearing it from someone else.

In my teens, I saw the human race riots on TV. That was scary, but it was happening halfway around the world to someone else, so I tried to forget about it. But trying to forget didn't erase the sick feeling in the pit of my stomach. The sense of waiting.

Helen is still my best friend, but she's now a lawyer. When the Allam killed that senator and the news exploded all over the airwaves, she advised me to lay low. "How?" I asked her helplessly. After a laundry list of advice, all of it untenable--quitting my job, retreating to my parents' cabin in the woods--I chose to continue on. What she was saying sounded alarmist--

crazy, even. Why should anything happen to me?

It took half a year before word of the roundups reached us. Three months after that, they came into my work. Half a dozen men, as if I would have done something violent if there hadn't been such overwhelming numbers. My tentacles burned bright green with embarrassment as they led me away and I could hear the snake-hissing sound of whispers following behind me.

What has she done? Is she a part of it? Is she a terrorist?

They separated us into cells, but forgot that we spoke by water. At a certain time of every night, we turned on the faucets and sent messages down the drains. I heard the echoes of my misery, my people crying and calling warning to others. I didn't know if we were heard, if the messages went as far as they needed to go.

Here came the man who spoke only in grunts and hissed words--my jailor. He let me out into the yard for fifteen minutes, a short time in the sun. I found messages scrawled in the dirt that looked like random hieroglyphics of curves to any human unversed in our writing.

Water call at 8PM.
Hettie K is looking for John C.
Here 100 days. Anyone longer?

The newspaper of the prison. I toyed with adding something, but had nothing of importance. I was searching for no one--I already knew my parents were here--and knew no one was searching for me.

Until I ran across the message. *Helen looking for Sally B.*

The guard barked at me, and I realized I'd been standing in one place in shock. Quickly, I scrawled *I'm here* under the original message before I was hustled back into the flickering artificial glow of the light bulb hanging above my cage.

The next day, a new message appeared, *Lawsuit for Allam release pending in state court.*

Who would have access to the outside world to learn such a thing? I wrote *Thanks,* for lack of anything else.

Weeks passed, but I read nothing more in the yard about myself. We got fish slop at every meal, and the running joke down the water pipe was that pets would be going hungry without the tinned cat food they were giving us. I was so sick of the salty metal taste of the food that I usually returned my plate half-full. I worried and I paced the sides of the six by eight cell. No windows. No fresh air except those precious fifteen minutes in the sun.

I lost count of months, but the weather was cooler by the time I heard news again in the yard. It had been raining, so the ground was not great and the messages tended to melt down and become unintelligible.

Hel-n won on app-al. Rele-se in fiv- day-.

I translated: *Helen won on appeal. Release in five days.*

I waited. A week went by. No news, and the door of my jail cell certainly didn't open and set me free.

The newspaper returned after a rainy few weeks. The air was turning colder, more crisp; if it snowed, we wouldn't be let out anymore. Allams could only tolerate so much cold, and even fifteen minutes outside during the winter was hard for us. Maybe that's what they'd do to get rid of us--simply open the doors, march us all out and leave us in the yard to catch the snowflakes as they drifted down. I could picture it. I'd seen countless movies, fascinated by the idea of snow, but had never seen it in person. Now, the thought was equally appealing and appalling. To see snow…

To die.

Helen case bumped to Supreme Court, I read.

After that, it was too cold to go outside, and we were kept indoors. I sang down the water pipes, but no one had news for me. Perhaps my nearest neighbors in the cells on either side of me had nothing to do with the news about my friend's case, the lawsuit that was working to free us.

Days were hard to count when constantly locked indoors. I missed things taken as commonplace--walking in the park, talking with my translator, touching living things. Our mechanical translators were the first things taken from us, so we were voiceless except when we spoke through the faucet water. I wondered if I were able to go outside, and if it were raining hard enough, I'd be able to shout through the sky. I spent days imagining this.

When the door opened again, I was so astonished at seeing the surly jailor reappear that I sat down on my bunk and stared at him. "Well, come on," he said and escorted me outside, as if he had just done it yesterday--not months before.

The first thing I saw on the dirt newspaper that day was: *Helen funeral. Shot in back.*

There are no mourning rites for Allams, no tears. I lie on my bunk and my heart is breaking. My best friend, my companion from school, the one person who has stuck by me throughout my life. The only one willing to risk her life to save mine--not just mine, but the lives of all of my kind.

Killed by one of hers.

So here is where I was at the beginning. I lie here and wonder about the Allam who put all of us into this jail. I lie here and wonder how the humans are going to kill us, now that our biggest advocate, and my best friend, is dead.

#

Days pass, and I lie on the bunk. I don't go out. I barely eat. I say nothing down the waterways.

Until the door opens and I hear a new voice, the first new voice I've heard in over a year other than my surly jailor. "Congratulations," it says.

I look up at the man in the doorway. I can't see him properly, as if a film has come over my eyes. I don't know what it is, because I can't cry, can't show the proper grief that Helen is due.

Maybe he expects a response from me, but I give him nothing. After clearing his throat, he says, "Sally. It's good news. You're free to go. Everyone's free."

Helen, I think. I get to my feet and walk through the door.

I wonder if this is how he felt--that Allam who killed. If he held such a rage in his heart that he could think of nothing else, do nothing but follow that rage through to the end.

Freedom from this prison is the first step on the path to finding Helen's killer. Where I will follow this path, don't ask me.

I don't know. Really, I just don't know.

Alison McBain is an award-winning and Pushcart Prize-nominated author with work in Flash Fiction Online, On Spec, and Abyss & Apex. Her debut novel The Rose Queen received the Gold Award for the YA fantasy category of the 2019 Literary Classics International Book Awards. When not writing, she is the associate editor for the literary magazine Scribes*MICRO*Fiction.

The Cauldron of Metamorphose
James Rowland

Eilidh sat with her puffins on the cliff and painted with the sea. Her legs dangled over the side, some fifty feet above the waves crashing against the rocks. She moved her hand through the wind. Reaching out, she shifted the sands beneath the sea. The waves split off in new directions and shapes. Her eyes turned up and the sky became dark and hazy, clouds as brushstrokes, creating the contrast for the vista she could see in her mind. What was left was a masterpiece, a chaotic swirling of blues and whites, dancing under the darkened skies. She admired it for a moment. She let the view sink into her memories. Then the magic fell away and nature reasserted itself, a servant no more. Eilidh smiled at the puffins around her, the birds looking up with their orange beaks, quizzical, silently wishing she would hurl fish from the sea. Laughing, Eilidh shook

her head and stood up. Not even her greatest spells, even the ones that gave the birds voices, or transformed them into all manner of companions, could distract them from their one true longing: food.

She left the puffins there perched on the cliff, waiting for their dinner, as she walked back to her hut. Atop the island, she heard the music first this time. Picking out the faint crashing symphony folded into the wind, Eilidh's body stiffened. She clenched her fists. The waves came crashing over her a moment later. Her breath froze in her throat. Her hair rose on end. Eilidh wrapped her arms tight around herself and tried to remember what warmth felt like. Another moment, her lungs burning, gasping for air, and the wave was gone. Eilidh stood alone on the hill on the island, on her island. She patted herself down, checking for any sign of the waves' embrace, wet fabric against her skin. She was dry. Like she always was after one of these strange attacks. Instinct demanded she check all the same.

Eilidh didn't understand the waves. Even now, she looked around the island. She stood on Staffa; a glorified rock hurled into the sea. It was true that the waves crashed against the shore and into the Cave below, but Eilidh wasn't there. She lived on the grassy surface that might as well have been the hair of some giant's head. The waves couldn't reach this high. Perhaps, it was just a part of her exile. A curse they had placed on her as they left her on the island and rowed away, condemning her banishment.

Taking a deep breath, her muscles relaxing, Eilidh continued her walk back to the hut nestled in the small valley on Staffa. It was sheltered from the wind, giving her a little comfort even in the bleakest winters. As modest as an honest monk, she had grown the hut from the weeds themselves. She reached out to the earth, wrapping herself around the strands. They grew. They fattened. The grassland shifted and took form, walls appearing from the ground. There was nothing inside it except a raised patch of soft vegetation, a bed for her to rest on. A cat sat on it. It was tiny, barely much more than a kitten, and its black fur was interrupted with patches of white and a dot of bright orange upon its nose. Eilidh wasn't sure how long her spell would maintain this form, but she was sure that all witches, banished or otherwise, needed a cat.

"How are my sisters?" the cat said.

Lowering her head, Eilidh walked inside and sat down on the bed. She sighed. "Hungry. Like usual. They didn't care about my painting."

"And did you bring back any fish?"

Eilidh rolled her eyes. "They said they would save you some."

"Perfect," the cat purred, sliding off the bed and out of the door in almost a single, graceful movement. Eilidh shook her head. You could remake the puffin into something else, but you couldn't change its heart's true desire. Maybe that was why she had never twisted their form into that of a human, to grow out its limbs and change its face until she had something more to keep her company than fish-obsessed birds and strange wave attacks. She wasn't sure she could take rejection in favour for the search of more trout.

Swinging her legs onto the bed, Eilidh laid back and stared up at the ceiling, weeds knotted together. When it was wet and cold, it was a grateful sight. Today, though, it felt like a prison. She hated it. She lifted a hand and flicked her wrist. The ceiling untied. Strands of grass slipped free of each other, suddenly eels, dancing away as the top of the hut opened up. The lingering, pale orange of the sunset hung above her and already the moon was taking its seat upon the pedestal of night. Eilidh smiled and sank into her bed of soft earth, watching as the colour drained away into darkness.

There were worse forms of punishments. Eilidh knew other girls in other villages hadn't been granted the gratitude and mercy of a banished life. When she was just a babe in her mother's arms, a witch had been pulled from her cottage, tied to the stake and then burnt for three days as the wind shrank from its task. Another had been tied with ball and chain while the men cut through the ice. They dropped her through the hole. The lake never unfroze. These women were snuffed from life. Eilidh relaxed in banishment. With her animals, she ruled her island. She was Circe reborn, a witch who made her prison her stately manor. She painted with the seas, she slept with skies, she walked across her windswept home and she played with her animal companions. It was hardly a punishment at all.

Men came sometimes too. They heard of the beautiful witch who ruled Staffa. Some men came with sails and Eilidh would watch them from her cliffs, slapped around by the winds. If she was feeling generous, she'd shift the currents just enough to give them safe passage back to the mainland. Often, she just watched them until the night swallowed the struggling figure. Those who rowed, though, would land on the beach. They'd take hold of their boat with strong hands and heave it up the sand. They knew better than to leave it bobbing in the sea. A boat will abandon its master with enough encouragement from the waves. Most of these men were ruffians, ready to pluck her from her home. Eilidh waited for them. They walked to her hut and she plucked them from the island. The winds came and wrapped its hand around their tiny bodies. They flew so far.

Occasionally, when the breeze was just right and the clouds vanished to leave the sun unmolested in the sky, real men came. They sat with her and talked. They hadn't meant to come to Staffa but were blown off-course. They found they liked the witch who ruled there. With red hair and skin so pale that it bordered on snow, they sat and shared stories with her. All of them were concerned she was malnourished, her arms and legs more like the branches of a tree, but she smiled and said she was well here. She enjoyed their company too, took them to her hut, and then left them to stare glass-eyed at the horizon as they sailed away the next day alone.

"What did you do?" one of these strangers said one day, sitting with her on the octagonal columns that led down to the sea crashing against the black basalt. His name was Douglass and he smelt like morning. "Why did they send you here?"

Eilidh laughed but it had no energy to make it further than her lips. She wanted to pretend that she didn't remember, that it had been so long ago and it was a trifling little thing, long forgotten in favour of her new life. She didn't care about her family retreating deeper into the shadows of memories. It didn't plague her that her mother's face was blurred, details swallowed by time. It wasn't true, though. She knew her crime and the punishment still stung. "I cured people. There was a plague, a disease of some sort, and people were dying in my village. I went out to each house. I did so at night to try and hide it. I knelt by each bed and I dragged the sickness from their bodies. I saved everyone I went to. Not a single person died. Not a single person saw me except those I cured."

The implication waited in the air for Douglass to grab it. "Someone you saved betrayed you?" Eilidh nodded. He shook his head. "But surely you should have been picked up and thrown onto people's shoulders, paraded through the village like a hero?"

She laughed again, this time with vigour. "You fishing boys are all the same. You know nothing of the world beyond your boats. The plague was God's will. More importantly, it was the will of the men that the plague was the work of God. They had deemed prayer sufficient. I offended God and I offended the men by going against them. I couldn't be allowed to stay. They took me from my home, they carried me down to the shore and loaded me into the nearest boat like a bag of grain. No arguments. No attempt at compromise. They left me here on this island before the sun had even finished brushing against the top of the sky. But it's fine. I like it here. It's peaceful. Quiet."

"I can take you with me. No one will know that you escaped your banishment.

My family lives alone by the sea, we barely see another soul except to trade what we can't make ourselves. You'll be happy. It's peaceful there too."

Sitting with the boy, barely a man, his skin freckled and his hair buckling under the force of the wind, Eilidh wanted to say yes. It sounded like a nice life, a pleasant one. She opened her mouth and found only one word escaping: no. The next day Douglass was gone. The next month, she wondered, with tears stinging her eyes, why she had rejected him. The next year, she barely remembered Douglass sitting on the basalt columns with her. It all fell away into the sea eventually.

Stars vanished, blinked out of existence as the inside of her eyelids replaced the sky. She could feel herself drifting away, sleep her only true companion. The waves came again. Even here, on the top of the island, in her little hut nestled in the bosom of the valley, the water came. It roared over her. Like a vagabond waiting outside the tavern for some coins to fleece, it roughed her up. Something punched her in the rib, like a boulder thrown up from the shore. The water rushed to fill her nose. A waterfall claimed her throat, pooling in her lungs. She coughed. Her body struggled to bring up the water. She rolled over, a thunderstorm in her ears, and she choked, nothing coming from her burning throat. She was going to die. And then, as fast as they came, the waves were gone. She was left on her bed of earth, as dry as a distant desert.

Eilidh slumped, her face pressed against the grass. She breathed in deeply. A voice in her head whimpered that the attacks were getting worse. She needed to find a way to stop them. The voice slipped away, becoming first an echo and then a memory as sleep came. It wrapped her in darkness and deposited her on the basalt columns that led to the Cave. She knew it

was a dream. A storm had brewed overnight and the rain and wind whipped around her and she felt nothing, only the absence of cold. She knew it was a dream because instead of turning around and fleeing back to the haven of the top of her island, she walked along the blackened columns and toward the Cave. A glow, warm, golden and flickering, seemed to fill it. It was waiting for her.

Even on the mainland, as a child listening to tall tales by the fireplace, Eilidh knew what had lived in that Cave. A monster lived there. As tall as three men and stronger than a dozen oxen, the giant Benandonner had ruled this island from the Cave. The basalt columns that Eilidh walked down were the ruins of the causeway that he himself had destroyed in his fight with a rival far across the sea. She knew that if there ever had been a giant, it would be long dead. Her head told her, in calm, reasoned tones, that giants weren't real and even if they were, the great Benandonner couldn't possibly live in such a small cave. There was nothing to fear there. Eilidh hadn't ventured down to the Cave anyway. Not yet. Not until tonight, safe in the knowledge that she was lighter than a feather, the collection of thoughts stitched together to make up a dream. She was safe in her hut on the top of the island.

Continuing along the columns, her feet moving from one to the next, her eyes wandered from the Cave to the Atlantic. It waited right next to her, nothing standing between her and the churning, black sea. The waves smashed against the side of the island. It reached out for her body. She remained just out of grasp. Sure-footed, the basalt smooth against her skin, she moved through the mouth of the Cave, its great top lip hovering above her. Her breath caught in her throat. A shiver started in her neck and danced down her spine. The Cave was illuminated by a sea of candles, floating through the air, suspended from the strands of her dream. Under their orange glow, Eilidh saw the basalt columns continuing, a staircase into the heart of the Cave. Beneath her, the water churned and crashed against the rocks, the floor of Benandonner's home just an extension of the Atlantic. There was no relief here.

Closing her eyes, the orange haze still seeping through, Eilidh breathed in and readied herself to wake up. This was enough exploring for today. Before she could end the dream, though, her heart stumbled off rhythm. She braced herself against the wall. Every muscle in her body went taut. She had heard it, the symphony of the waves crashing over to drown her, another attack reaching her even in sleep. She waited. She stood frozen on her little ledge. Seconds passed. The attack never came. Opening her eyes, Eilidh shuffled to the edge of the steps and glanced down into the churning water. The sound that stalked her across the island bubbled up from below.

The only thing Eilidh could hear in her little hut as she woke was the thundering of her own heart.

For a week, she tried to distract herself with other things. She marched down to the cliff and spun out voices for every puffin in reach. They croaked of fish and of fine breezes for flying. Conversation was beyond them. She took some of them and grew them into other pets, a menagerie of black, white and orange furs as cats, rabbits and dogs dominated the island. They would talk to her. They could even hold her attention for more than a few minutes at a time. It still wasn't enough to stop her thoughts turning back to the Cave. The attacks kept coming. She kicked out at the earth as another wave struck her from the top of the island. She screamed. It was endless. She marched from one end of Staffa to another in an afternoon, pausing

to call the grass up. It stretched higher and higher, strands winding together, growing stronger, becoming fleshy, green lighthouses that dotted the landscape. She ran out of land all too soon. Banishment had finally snapped. Its teeth sank deep into her flesh. It left bitemarks in her sanity. There was only one thing she could do.

She waited until the clouds had parted. Descending into the Cave, where giants were said to live, and her curse seemed to draw power from, was already foreboding enough. She did not need the weather to provide further assistance. When the suffocating greyness did yield, though, Staffa looked beautiful in the midday sun. The island was bathed in light. Eilidh took her time to head down to the basalt columns and the Cave beyond. Sitting with the puffins, watching them battle the ever-present wind in their search for fish, her breathing steadied. She reached out to one bird and ran a finger along its back. It didn't move. It didn't take flight. When she stood up, though, her friends all took to the air and began to sing. They twisted and turned, flying in rhythm, a beat emerging as the flock took shape. A shimmering, curling spiral took to the air. It almost glinted in and out of sight. Eilidh couldn't escape the idea they were waving goodbye to her. She bit her lip and offered her own wave before walking away.

Eilidh's heart began its migration to her mouth as she walked to the Cave. In her dream, the weather was wet and wild, a villain lurching out from the shadows, but she knew the sea it worked with was toothless. She could not die. It was just a dream. Now, things were different. The waves still crashed against the edge of the island, rising up over the nearest columns. Eilidh walked higher up, pressed up tight against the cliff face. Each step was a knife, though. Each column frayed the edges of her nerves a little more. She wasn't sure how much further she could go before it snapped completely. All she could see was her foot slipping on the basalt, her body tumbling down toward the Atlantic, the waves snarling and striking out to grab her, her life disappearing into the sea. But she arrived at the mouth of the Cave without incident. Her island would not betray her.

The Cave was as beautiful in the day as it was in the dream-logic of night where it bathed in an orange haze. Eilidh continued to scramble across the columns, pushing deeper as the blueish green water churned and bubbled beneath her, crashing into the rocks. She looked down. For just a heartbeat, she thought of a witch and some cauldron. Maybe this was how she was being cursed. She frowned, swallowing back the urge to kick out at the column in front of her. It was nonsense. Witches didn't sit around in pointy hats, brewing potions over large, bubbling cauldrons. She knew that. It was just the shape stories needed to be to scare the right people. Somehow, somewhere, at some moment, the message had lodged deep inside the crevices of even her brain. The thought burned inside her. It gave her fuel to push further inside the darkening Cave.

The music of her attacks walked alongside her now, a constant companion. There was no doubt left inside her. The water crashing against the rocks was what Eilidh could hear just before she would be hit by the dry waves, pinning her down, forcing her to drown. She could hear her heart up in her ears now, a steady beating drum as she knew she was drawing closer to unravelling the mystery. The idea that there would be nothing awaiting her sat beyond the horizon of understanding. Eilidh could feel it in her bones. She was going to find her answers. A dozen images ran through her mind, cursed jewels and

walls of herbs. She didn't expect to see the body.

Eilidh froze deep inside the Cave. She could smell the salt in the air, the spray stinging her eyes. In the darkness, she thought it might be her own shadow cast against the wall. Another step closer, though, revealed the chains. Her eyes followed them from the body, wrapped around the ankles and wrists, turning the figure into a star, and then snaked up the cave wall. The path ended with the chains looped around great metal rods, hammered into the rock itself. Eilidh tried to swallow, but even the muscles in her throat had turned to stone. She eyed the metal rods. She pictured men sailing into the Cave, climbing the columns, dealing with the wind and water, clinging to safety as they drove heavy iron bars into the very heart of the stone itself. It was a task worthy of song. Eilidh couldn't help but wonder what powerful evil must have led to those men taking such drastic action.

Rooted to the spot, she felt a tugging on her hands, both forward and back. Eilidh knew she could walk away. On the surface of Staffa, she could live with her puffins and her hut, and as Circe of the North, she could grow old in the playground of her own power. The attacks would continue to come, though. The waves would continue to swallow her. She needed answers. Eilidh took a step forward and then another. Her hands shook and her legs descended into the consistency of porridge, barely able to support her weight. They wanted to crumple beneath her. They wanted to throw her into the water below rather than confront the ancient evil chained to the wall. Though her body tried to betray her, Eilidh's mind and soul was as one, pushing through the sticky, clenching fingers of fear.

The closer she came to the body, the more it fell out of shadows. It sat outside the shape that Eilidh had built for it, tall and strong. Instead, she saw something short and slight, the figure slumped with its chin on its chest. Its dirty, knotted, red hair covered whatever face might exist behind the curtain. Eilidh noticed, with a gasp, the suggestion of breasts under that chin. She had expected a demon or a giant, not a woman. The woman on the wall was so pale that she bordered on snow and limbs seemed not much more than the weakest, undernourished branches of a tree. At Eilidh's approach, the woman lifted her head. Her hair fell back from her face to reveal skin drawn too tight over bone; lines etched deep into the surface. Whatever colour that might have existed was drained completely. It was Eilidh's face.

She had just enough time to scream and then the waves came and washed her away from the basalt columns and into the sea.

Eilidh opened her eyes in stages. The salt-encrusted grime tried to keep them shut, yielding in tactical retreats until she was finally able to see the Cave in front of her. She looked out and saw the suggestion of an existence beyond it, a world that hid just out of reach. Every inch of her arms and legs burned. Her muscles screamed in protest, stretched to their limits. There was nothing she could do about that. Her head lolled to the side and looked at the great metal rods buried inside the rock, holding her chains in place. She tried to groan in pain or protest, she wasn't sure which, but her throat refused to engage. She couldn't even move her tongue. Pinned to the cave wall, looking down at her prison, she wondered if it was just numb or if she even had a tongue anymore. She couldn't check.

Despite the agony, the cold, the numbness, the burning and the sheer exhaustion stitched into every part of her

body, Eilidh knew what had happened. She didn't need to let the realisation sink in. It was already in her heart. She hadn't been Circe. It had been an illusion, a way for the shattered pieces of her mind to cope with the truth. She had never been Circe. Why would men reward her actions with freedom? It was the last thing of all that a man would offer. Instead, she was Prometheus and this was her real punishment. There was no liberation here, only chains. There was no magic to experiment with, only the stranglehold of boredom and pain. There were no puffins as friends, only two Great Skua, dark birds waiting to see if their newest feast was yet prepared. Her movement meant it was not. They took flight, but they would be back soon. It couldn't be long now.

But the illusion had brought her time. She had survived longer than they were expecting, birds or men. The chains felt weaker, screaming as she struggled against them. Just as Prometheus, she could not be chained here forever. She would escape. Eilidh braced herself as the tide surged forward. She heard the melody of the Cave, and then the waves crashed over her chained body. She could outlast them.

James Rowland *is a New Zealand-based, British-born writer. His work has previously appeared at Aurealis, Compelling Science Fiction, and Prairie Fire. When he's not moonlighting as a writer of magical, strange or futuristic stories, he works as an intellectual property lawyer. Besides writing, his hobbies are reading, travel, photography, and the sport of kings, cricket. You can find more of his work at his website https://www.jamesrowland.net/*

Crazy Ezzo

Chris Cornetto

A prickling rain spills from slate-gray clouds, little needles whipped to a fury by the gusting wind. It lashes from all sides, plastering clothes to skin and soaking every inch.

Nico's hair clings to his face, water trailing from it in streamers. He brushes it aside, but the wind blows it right back. He hugs his ribs to keep from shivering. The angry sea froths against the pier, hungry for him.

He hates the sea. Hates the very thought of sailing. Ships are little bugs that crawl across the roiling flesh of Sepha. All a sailor can do is pray not to tickle, not to disturb, lest the god notice him.

"Move it!" calls the man with the whip, shouting against the wind. He lashes the prisoners at the rear of the pack, spurring them into those ahead. Collisions ripple up the line waiting to board.

Nico is shoved forward. He staggers on the rain-slick quay, clumsy from the chains on his ankles. As he teeters on the brink, the inky waves surge, reaching out for him. He screams.

A hand catches him. His body trembles from more than the cold.

"Someone's got the jitters!" says Crazy Ezzo, bracing Nico's shoulder. "Tryin' to sail without the ship, eh?" He cackles like a loon.

Ezzo *always* cackles.

Nico brushes the man's hand away. "I'm fine," he snaps, though he is not fine at all. He is, in fact, going to die. The god Sepha is waiting for him.

Ezzo shrugs and grins his stupid grin, the rain streaking his grimy face. "Cheer up, sourpuss. Shake them barnacles from your britches! It's a lovely day!"

Dassus, the hulking lizardman, looks over his shoulder. He rolls his reptilian eyes.

Ahead, the galley *Permarina* rocks in the churning surf. It's a long three-master, built for trade but capable in a fight. The line of sodden indentures trudges toward it, their chains clanking a dissonant tune.

Indenture, Nico thinks wryly. *Just a kinder name for slavery.*

The chain tugs, and Nico takes a few more steps. He dreads his turn to board. Dark waves lap at the pier like Sepha's cruel laughter, inviting him to the god's embrace. His knees go weak.

It isn't death he fears, but the manner of it. Drowning terrifies him.

He forces his gaze away from the water, fixing on the ship until his tremors ease. Such bitter irony that the *Permarina*, his prison, should also be his comfort.

Ezzo catches him staring at the galley. "Not a bad ship. I've seen worse." He shrugs. "Sailed on worse."

Dassus hisses. He shakes his head and spits into the surf.

"Well, I didn't call it a *good* ship!" Ezzo shouts back. He laughs with childlike glee.

"It's a floating coffin," Nico mutters to himself.

Somehow Ezzo hears him over the gale. "Might just be," he agrees. "Let's hope them coffin-nails are tight enough to keep the fishies out." He winks and giggles again.

Nico doesn't see the humor.

The line of prisoners pauses. Dassus nudges Ezzo and nods toward the ship. He gives a long hiss, punctuated by consonants and clicks.

Ezzo shakes his head, flinging water from his beard. He rubs the rain from his eyes and stares at the mast. His face lights up. "Right you are!" he tells the lizardman. "Bad news for us, I guess."

Nico leans forward, curiosity mingling with his fear. "What's bad news?" he asks. No one answers.

The line picks up and they shuffle toward the ship, getting close now. Dassus inclines his head to where indentures march up the gangway, then points at his own irons. He gives Ezzo a meaningful look and hisses something to him.

"Yep, that too," Ezzo says, cackling. "Oh, we're in for it good!"

"What's bad news?" Nico shouts again. The wind howls, trying to drown him out.

Ezzo gives him a gap-toothed grin. He points up at the pennants snapping in the breeze. "See? City colors, but no house flag."

Nico strains his eyes against the pelting rain. Ravencourt colors, a black chevron on a field of white. "So?" Any merchant could rent a ship from the city. Why should a dead man care whose ship carries him to the grave?

"And there's no volunteers. Get it?" Ezzo grins and nudges him. "Just a bunch of chain-legs like us. Hoo-ee, it's gonna be a trip, eh?" He breaks into another fit of giggles.

Nico looks up and down the line. Ezzo is right. Normally, most oarsmen row for wages and the right to transport cargo – an honest living for anyone fool enough to go to sea. His grandfather had done the same.

The lack of volunteers *is* odd, but Nico doesn't care. So what if he drowns among debtors and criminals? Would the screams of freemen comfort him when the sea takes them all?

A wave slaps the pier, misting him with spray that makes him no wetter. He turns his head away from the driving rain. So do all the others.

All except Crazy Ezzo. He cups his hands and cries into the storm. "So long, land! So long, city! Might be I'll see you again sometime!" A guard grabs his elbow and steers him up the plank.

Nico, bound to him by the chain on his ankle, follows onto the ramp. He staggers as the plank bucks beneath him, threatening to heave him into the sea before he even reaches the ship. The man behind him curses and shoves him forward.

Crazy Ezzo peeks over his shoulder. "Then again, maybe not, eh?" He winks.

Before he steps aboard, Nico steals one last glance at the thrashing waves, weighing the mercy of a quick, painful death.

Niccolo Forza didn't always hate the sea.

He owned many ships, once, though he'd never sailed one. He had wanted to be a captain, but that changed too. Life is full of twists.

The second son of a wealthy merchant, Nico was expected from birth to be a priest of Sepha. It was a way to honor the god and bring prestige to the family. More importantly, it was a way to avoid dividing wealth among an ever-branching family tree. Daughters could be dowered off, an acceptable one-time expense, but sons were harder. Sons expected to be heirs.

But young Nico didn't covet the family fortune. It was the sea he loved, the freedom it promised. It made his heart ache to see his brother Teo always at father's side, learning the business he would one day inherit. Each time they prepared to sail, Nico would beg to come with them. And every time, father sent him back to his tutors.

Every time, except for the last one.

Nico had thought himself clever when he realized he could use his mother to pull father's strings. For weeks, he implored her to speak with father. Just one adventure, he begged. One chance to see the world before he was trapped inside the temple walls. What harm could it do?

To everyone's surprise, father relented. Nico would finish his studies, and, on the next voyage, he could come along. After all, what harm could it do?

But the next voyage never came. Father and Teo died at sea, wrecked without even a storm. It happened sometimes.

Mother, a devout woman, blamed herself. She had tricked her husband into offending the god, and thus sent him to a watery grave. Within a month, she climbed the cliffs west of town and joined her husband in the sea.

That was when the nightmares began.

By the time the rowers are chained to their benches, the worst of the storm has passed. Still the ship rocks and heaves.

If Nico had anything in his stomach, he would have lost it. Sour bile creeps up his throat.

"Lookin' a mite green," notes Ezzo, chained next to him. The madman is, if anything, more cheerful than ever. He is infuriating. "I can hardly tell you from Dassus!"

The giant lizardman chuckles. Neither he nor Ezzo shows any discomfort. Nico hates them for it.

The three of them share an oar. Most oars have four men working them, but Dassus counts for two. Stroke by stroke, they drag the lurching ship clear of the harbor.

Together they row in endless rhythm. Lift and push, dip and pull, over and over. The galley crawls forward like a scurrying bug. Time passes.

Eventually the drum falls silent and the rowers stop, not a moment too soon for Nico. His back aches, his hands are raw with blisters, and they're only a few hours into the voyage. He wonders if he'll die of exhaustion before the god can claim him, but knows he's not so lucky.

"Chow time!" Ezzo hoots. "Best time of the day!"

Wind whistles in the oar ports, and through them Nico sees the daylight fade to red. The coast floats past in the distance.

A boy comes around with a bucket and ladle, bringing water to the crew. Nico's parched throat aches for it. After an age, his turn comes; he takes a sip and grimaces. The water is sour, but he downs it all.

Ezzo giggles at him. "They mix in a little wine, if you can call it that." He drinks a scoop with relish, then passes one to Dassus. "More like vinegar, eh? But beggars can't be choosers if they want to be boozers!"

Dassus glares at the water boy, holds up two claw-tipped fingers, and hisses something in his lizard-tongue. Instead of returning the ladle, he hands it to Ezzo.

"My friend says he gets more water," Ezzo translates, "because he's big. Also, because he's good at pulling arms off." He gives the boy the ladle with a broad, friendly grin.

Dassus grins, too, but there's nothing warm in his rows of razor-teeth.

The boy, hands shaking, gives the lizardman a second scoop. When he comes back later with bread, Dassus doesn't need to ask for an extra loaf.

Nico almost feels bad for the kid, but his pity is reserved for himself. By the time he finishes gnawing the hard bread, it is full dark. He slumps with his face in his hands, wondering how he will manage to sleep with nowhere to lie.

And, while he ponders, his body finds a way.

In his dreams, as always, the sea stretches all around him. He treads water until he can't, until his muscles seize and fail. First one wave, then another, closes over his head until cold water enfolds him like a shroud. The gray sky drifts away and fades to black. Salty brine fills his aching, desperate lungs. All around are the twisting, writhing leviathans, children of the god. They swim past him, watching with their lantern eyes, their dagger teeth...

He screams, but does not wake.

#

Niccolo Forza was not a fool. Though he had been training for the clergy, he had a head for numbers. He understood commerce. By all rights, business should have flourished under his guidance.

It might have, if he didn't keep losing ships.

There were factors he simply couldn't control. An unexpected storm, an attack by pirates. Rumors, unconfirmed, of a leviathan. His fleet dwindled by the year, and his fortune with it. People called him Nico the Cursed.

It became hard to find captains willing to sail for him, even for outrageous pay. People asked, and rightly so, why he wouldn't lead his own expeditions. If they could have seen the monsters that snaked through the nightmare depths of his dreams, they would have understood his terror. Going to sea was not an option.

Instead he went to the Grand Temple of Sepha, to ask the priests to intercede for him. Gold, they said, would please the god. He gave and gave again, but still his vessels foundered.

Sepha clearly wanted more.

It is still dark when the drummer shouts for them to rise.

Nico wakes, embarrassed to find his head on Ezzo's shoulder. Ezzo leans on Dassus, who sits there like a scaly, green hill. All through the ship, rowers slumped in similar piles rise and stretch out their stiffness.

Nico's hands sting and his muscles ache, but he no longer feels the rocking of the ship. Outside, the wind is still and silent, the god's attention elsewhere. For now.

The guards take the rowers, a bench at a time, up to the deck. When Nico's turn comes, he pisses over the rail for what feels like an hour. Despite Ezzo's stench, the air

39

is fresh and sharp. The full moon is bright on the waves, but storm clouds loom ahead.

If Nico jumped from the ship, met his death like a man, the others might be spared his fate. But he is too much a coward.

Besides, he would never reach the water. He'd only hang from his chains like a fool, dangling from the foot of Mount Dassus.

Ezzo tugs up his breeches and squints into the distance. He whistles through his teeth. "Watcha think? See those spines? Hoo-ee. A real shipbreaker, that one!"

Nico doesn't look, for fear he'll see spines crest the surf in every wave – the monsters of his nightmares invading his waking life. The breeze, pleasant moments ago, turns uncomfortably cold. He is almost relieved to return below deck.

Chained back to the bench, they row until dawn. With dawn comes another meal, a surprise of extra rations. Several rowers cheer

But, for a moment, Ezzo looks nervous. The madman catches Nico watching him and breaks instantly into his lunatic grin. "Lucky us, eh? Better see if we can get some moldy loaves."

Nico thinks the man is joking, but he's not. Ezzo really trades his loaf – stale, but perfectly edible – for the worst of the batch. After leaving a few crumbs on the floor, a strange ritual of his, he bites into the gray, fuzzy bread with such enthusiasm that it makes Nico want to vomit. He nearly does.

Nico looks at Dassus, gestures to Ezzo. "Do you see this?" he wants to shout. "Do you see what kind of idiot we're chained to?" The lizardman only shrugs.

Nico chokes down his bread, chokes down his disgust. It doesn't matter, he tells himself. They'll all be dead soon, anyway.

The wind is weak this morning, so there is rowing to be done. Nico throws himself into the labor, losing himself in the rhythm. He disappears into his thoughts. Strangely, he finds something else among the fear and self-pity. He is curious.

"Ezzo, why did you ask for moldy bread?"

Crazy Ezzo smiles his gap-toothed grin. "Because there's *double* rations. Don't you see?" He looks around the ship, face pale and eyes fever-bright. He is clammy with sweat, but so are they all.

"Also," he adds softly, "the rats told me 'bout the cargo."

"The rats!" Nico shakes his head in irritation, though it's his own fault for expecting sense from a madman. "Do *not* tell me you talk to rats." Ezzo opens his mouth, but Nico shushes him. "Don't. I don't want to hear it."

"Talk to rats..." Ezzo mutters, chuckling softly. "Of course I don't talk to rats! That would be crazy."

Nico nods and lets the matter drop. He turns his attention back to rowing, eager to end the conversation he'd foolishly started.

Without missing a stroke of the oar, Ezzo leans so close that his breath makes Nico's eyes water. "The rats, you see," he whispers, "*they* talk to *me*." He bursts into a fit of giggles.

Nico's annoyance erupts into fury. With no concern for the galley master's lashes, he reaches for Ezzo's throat.

His hand is barely off the oar when Dassus catches his wrist and forces it back.

Nico thrashes angrily, but the lizardman's grip is iron. "Let me go! I'll row! I just need to strangle him first!"

Dassus waits for Nico to calm before letting go. He points to the floor at Ezzo's feet.

The crumbs are gone. In their place are fish bones and a shred of dyed wool.

"See?" Ezzo asks cheerfully, oblivious to Nico's rage. "Cargo."

Niccolo Forza had been at his wits' end. No matter how cautious the routes he chose for his ships, no matter how well they were guarded, disaster found them. When his very last ship crawled into port, one mast cracked and half its oars missing, he knew he was ruined.

The galliot *Undine* was a light escort ship, carrying more soldiers than cargo. Nico had gathered his last ships into a convoy for safety. Each of the captains demanded triple wages for the danger they risked, and he had agreed. It proved a foolish bargain on their part. They were dead, their cargo and crew taken by slavers.

Nico had nothing left. He had sold off his inventory, then his warehouses. He sold the furniture from his home until it was a shell. Even the house itself was collateral on a loan he would soon default on.

Nico, once a cautious boy, had grown into a doubly cautious man. It was therefore to everyone's surprise when he stormed into the Temple of Sepha and assaulted the high priest.

The storm ahead gives them a miss, and the next day's rowing is peaceful. Two more days pass much the same.

Though Nico knows the god is playing with him, he can't help but hope. Maybe he'll survive the journey? Maybe he'll live long enough to work off his indenture? If he does, he'll sell the *Undine* and start over, far, far from the sea – something he should have done years ago.

Of course, if he sold his last ship, it would mean admitting defeat. He never did know when to give up.

Nico is sore, but it's bearable. He feels his body adapting to the strain of rowing, feels his motion become more fluid. The comfort of his old life melts from his frame, revealing muscle beneath the softness.

While Nico grows stronger, Ezzo weakens. The man needs the chamber pot routinely, shitting his guts out by the hour. His stench is unbearable.

But, no matter how sick he is, Crazy Ezzo requests the worst rations and eats them with glee. If not for his attitude, obnoxiously cheery, Nico would swear the man wished for death.

To Nico's surprise, he pities the man. Ironically, his own desire to die has grown less urgent.

In a perverse way, the rowing is almost enjoyable. His fate is not in his hands. There are no decisions to make, nothing to plan for. The future is full of disaster, but it's not on him to avert it.

Not that he could if he tried.

But throughout this meditation, a thought nags at him. Ezzo, crazy as he is, was right about something. The ship is carrying the wrong cargo.

They are sailing north; the sun makes that much obvious. The ship carries fish and wool, perhaps glass, too. Ravencourt glass is the best in the world – because it turns a profit in any port, most ships bring at least some. Wool sells better in the east, but it could be packing for the glass. It's best to use packing that can also be sold.

The fish, though, makes no sense. Fish are plenty abundant in the warm waters of the north, and, even salted, need to be transported with haste. Such a perishable cargo would explain the speed of their journey, except that it's scarcely worth the cost of transporting.

Which leads Nico to the real problem. The *Permarina* is built for speed, and speed means rowers. But, as with everything, speed comes at a price. The space for rowers cuts into room for cargo – especially because rowers need to be fed. With every bench filled, and double rations for all, they should have stopped at least once by now to resupply. To keep sailing with no stops,

41

most of the hold must be filled with food and water.

What kind of merchant carries low value goods in too little bulk to turn a profit?

There is, of course, only one explanation: the listed goods are cover for some other cargo, carried discreetly. Something more profitable than legal.

As the pieces slide into place, Nico turns to Ezzo in triumph. "Ezzo, I get it now. I figured it out."

"Well, it's about time! Good on you." Though the man smiles, his face is pale and drawn, a waxen skull. He takes a hand off the oar to scratch his head. "So, um… watcha get?"

"The clues!" Nico nearly shouts. "Why the ship carries no house flag. Why there are no freeman rowers. Why we carry the wrong cargo. It all fits together!"

"Well, now. I'll bet it does." He tries to hide a grimace as his stomach gives a menacing gurgle.

For the first time, Nico wishes the man were more attentive. "Seriously, I get what you've been hinting. We're rowing for smugglers, aren't we?"

"That's some sharp thinkin' you did there!" Ezzo beams and pats him on the shoulder with a calloused, grimy hand. "Not right, but sharp."

Dassus gives a hissing chuckle.

Nico feels his cheeks bloom red with anger. Not right? Of course he's right! And yet the moron and lizard snicker at him, as if he's still on the outside of their little joke. He'd kill them both, if they weren't–

"You forgot about the extra rations," Ezzo says, interrupting the thought. "Which reminds me–" His voice cuts off in a croak and he scrunches up his face. "Shit pot, over here! Shit… oh, hells with it. Comin' through!" He slips his leg, skeleton-thin, free from the shackle and takes off running for the hatch. The guards are too shocked to stop him.

Dassus breaks into a laugh, a deep throaty rumble. He hisses and clicks something to Nico, but the words mean nothing. He is not even listening.

Extra rations. It makes no sense for smugglers to give them extra rations.

Damn the lunatic. Did he have to be right about everything?

Above, sailors begin to shout. Footsteps thump across the deck in a flurry of activity. At first Nico assumes Ezzo riled them, but the ship begins to rock. Thunder rolls in the distance. They are sailing into a storm.

By the time Ezzo scuttles back into the hold, the ship is bouncing across breakers. The wind howls, and spray mists through the oar ports. The patter of rain on the deck soon grows to a violent drumming as the storm begins in earnest. Water leaks through the planking to pool at Nico's feet.

Crazy Ezzo slips his leg back into the shackle and helps them draw in the oar. He tries to smile, but his eyes are wide and afraid. "Damn thing came on fast. Little too fast, eh?" His giggle is thin and nervous this time. "Never seen a storm do that. Every day at sea's an adventure, eh?"

As always, he is right. The storm is too sudden. The sails are not down fast enough, and they snap angrily in the gale. The masts creak with strain.

Thunder cracks loud enough to make Nico's ears ring. His skin tingles, and his hair stands on end.

"Hoo-ee!" Ezzo cries. "That'll wake the neighbors!" He laughs again, tries to smile at Dassus, but the expression slides from his face. Even the lizardman looks uneasy.

Nico knows they are right to be afraid.

"Ezzo, Dassus… This might be the wrong time, but I have a confession."

"Gold?" shouted Niccolo Forza. "Gold to please the god? Well, here's the last of it!"

And with that, he took off his family signet and threw it at the priest. Besides one broken-down ship he was too poor to fix, it was his last possession of worth.

The worshippers stared in horror as he denounced the priests. He named them liars, cheats, and charlatans. In the temple dome itself, surrounded by centuries-old mosaics of the god in his glory, he cursed Sepha himself for taking his family and fortune.

The priests tried to restrain him, but fury gave him strength. He shook them off and struck them. He kicked the altar, flung the gold ornaments aside. He toppled a brazier and set light to the rich azure carpet.

Then came the Templars. They bore him roughly to the ground, pinned him beneath their bulk. He bit and scratched and howled like a wild thing until his strength was spent.

There, in sight of the god, the high priest cursed his name. The priest condemned him, Niccolo Forza, to the everlasting wrath of Sepha.

The priest's eye, Nico noted with satisfaction, was swollen shut.

After a long stay in jail and a short trial, Nico's fine was set too high to pay. The temple ensured it was so. With no other recourse, he was indentured to row on the *Permarina*.

"Why are you *laughing*?" Nico shouts over the raging gale. "What do you *idiots* find so funny?" The ship bucks and heaves like an angry bull, nearly tossing him from his seat.

Ezzo bounces into the air and strikes the bench hard, but still he laughs. Dassus snickers until he snorts. The lizardman hisses something in his bestial tongue.

"Well?" Nico shouts again. They won't be laughing when the sea swallows them.

"Dassus says you deserve your curse," Ezzo says, "if you don't have the wits to break it." He hoots with laughter as the ship rolls over another wave.

"Break it?" Nico feels his face go hot with anger. "Are you stupid as well as mad? The *high priest* cursed my name! What the hells can I do against power like that?"

Again the morons laugh, as if they weren't doomed with him. The hull shudders, likely raking against a reef. It won't be long now.

The lizardman spews more meaningless hisses and clicks, and Ezzo breaks into a new fit of giggles. "Hah, true!" agrees the madman. "Pretty obvious, when you think about it."

"What's true? What's obvious?"

"How to break your curse, of course. Don't you see?"

With a loud crash, the ship shudders from an impact. It lists sharply, tossing the rowers to one side.

Nico lurches into Ezzo, smashing him against the lizardman. "No! I don't see!" he shouts into the lunatic's stupid grin. "Enough of your damned riddles! Tell me, damn you, before we all die!"

Crazy Ezzo only giggles more. "I can't. Wouldn't be fair."

"Fair? I'll show you fair!" As Nico reaches to throttle the madman, the ship tilts suddenly the other way, tossing him to the floor. He splashes into water, already knee-deep. "Fine! What's not fair?"

Ezzo offers a hand to help him back to the bench, and Nico takes it. "Dassus figured it out. You have to ask <u>him</u> the secret."

"But I don't understand his…" Nico stops. It doesn't matter. He shakes the water from his hair, wipes his face, and starts over. "Never mind. Fine." He'll play along now, strangle them both later – if anyone lives that long. "Dassus, tell me how to break the curse."

Dassus shakes his head and grins. His teeth are yellow knives.

"Aw, c'mon," Ezzo says. "You gotta ask nicer than that!"

The ship strikes something *hard*. Wood groans and cracks. Outside, angry thunder booms. Water pours in from the hatch, from between the planking in the deck. The fierce rain is a second sea, falling to crush them against the one below. It is Nico's every nightmare of the past eight years, and he *cannot wake*.

Nico's fury dissolves, pushed aside by soul-crushing terror. "Please!" he screams, his heart pounding against his ribs. "Please! I'll give you anything! I'll give you my last ship! Anything!"

Dassus hisses something, but Nico cannot hear it over the roaring storm.

Ezzo nods to the lizardman, turns to Nico. "It's easy-peasy," he says with a grin. "The priest cursed your name, right? So…?"

Nico waves his hand frantically, urging the madman to speak. Time is short.

Ezzo gives him a broad, gap-toothed smile. "So, all you've gotta do is change your name." He winks.

At that moment, the whole ship shakes. The hull bursts open aft of Dassus, and the rowers behind them are pulled screaming into the sea, their chain snapped free of the bench. Outside is midnight black.

Brilliant lightning rips across the sky, lighting lantern eyes, dagger teeth – a nightmare come to life. Nico's heart nearly stops.

There is no reef. A leviathan is attacking the ship. The god has come for him at last.

The ship fills with cries of fear and despair, some of them his own. Waist-deep brine sloshes in and out of the gap in the hull. The monster writhes alongside the ship, its spines scraping against it. It raises its tail and smashes down, splintering more wood. The ship heaves beneath its weight.

The ship tilts, and water rushes past them. Dassus hisses an urgent command.

Somehow, Nico understands it. He grabs up armfuls of chain, digging his fingers into the heavy links, taking up all the slack he can. Ezzo, cackling madly, does the same.

The ship bobs and swings the other way. The water that spilled past surges back at them, deeper than before. Nico gasps for breath as it washes over his head, as it stings his eyes and forces its way up his nose. The current tears at him, the god's grasping hands dragging him to the hungry deep. Death swirls all around him – the death that has stalked him for years.

Nico opens his eyes beneath the dark water. The god surrounds him, coursing over him in a cold, ripping current. It pulls him toward the waiting abyss. It demands his body, the very breath from his lungs. It demands his utter surrender.

"No," Nico whispers. The word is a bubble that tickles its way up his face. Still the current rages. "No!" he shouts, his pathetic defiance a waste of precious air. "You've taken everything, but you *can't have me!*"

He knits his fingers into the chain. It twists and chafes them, tries to writhe free, but he holds it fast. The sea rips and drags at him with a fury, refusing to be denied.

But Nico is stronger. His hands, hardened by labor at the oar, cling to the chain, his only tether to the world of the living. His muscles ache and his lungs scream for air.

After an eternity, the water recedes, and his head breaks the surface. Somehow, he is still on the ship.

Nico gulps air into stinging lungs, coughing and sputtering with every ragged breath. His eyes burn too much to see, but he can hear the water gush from the breach in the hull, can hear the crash of debris and the screams of men, dragged to the monster outside. Their wails give way to silence.

"Sepha!" he shouts through laughter and tears. He shakes his fist at the roaring sea. "Sepha! I'm still here, you bastard!" He giggles insanely, too giddy with relief to stop. "You didn't get me! I'm still here!"

His vision clears in time to see the leviathan drift away, glutted from its bloody feast. Several benches now sit empty.

So does the seat next to him. Ezzo is gone.

The storm departs as quickly as it struck. With no way to gauge direction, the ship bobs helplessly through the night, then limps to shore at dawn. The sailors wait for high tide to beach the ship. It takes two days to repair.

Nico says not a word in this time, merely passes the days lying in the sand. He is empty, spent, no longer himself. The man he used to be was swept away, devoured by the sea. What is left of him has been scoured clean by salty brine.

When the time comes to leave, some rowers refuse to board. The guards kill one and toss him into the waves; the rest comply. Indentures have rights, but only in harbor.

Nico understands their fear, but does not share it. The sea holds no more terror for him. He knows that Sepha will never find him, because he is no longer Nico. He has become something new.

He climbs the gangplank and finds his bench, not troubled by a care in the world. He passes over his old seat and takes the one next to Dassus, a gift left to him by the old man. He runs his hands through the mangy beard that's taken root on his face. Clarity floods him, transforms him.

He understands the *Permarina's* secret, the great cosmic joke. He knows the ship's contraband, the illegal cargo hidden by a hold of worthless fish. His heart is so full of laughter that he does laugh, just for the sound of it.

Dassus quirks a brow at him.

"Hoo-ee," Ezzo says. "That was one mean fishie! But we'll be in for worse at port, eh?"

The lizardman gives him a broad, toothy grin. "Sure will," he agrees in his hissing, clicking speech. "But there are days enough left to make yourself sick."

The man nods. Now that he is Ezzo, he *does* see. The unmarked ship and the indentures, the large crew and the cheap goods. Even the extra rations. The pieces fit together so well, it's a wonder he took so long to assemble them.

The crew *is* the cargo. Despite the laws of Ravencourt, they are sailing to a slave port to sell free men. But they will only sell the most valuable, and keep a skeleton crew to sail the ship home.

A skeleton crew, crewed by a living skeleton if Ezzo plays his cards right. "Guess I'd better cultivate a taste for mold, eh?" He giggles at his own wit.

Dassus nods. "You'd better. When we get home, you owe me a ship."

The drummer strikes up a rhythm. Together, they dip their oar into the surf, and pull.

Chris Cornetto *is a physics teacher by day and writer by night. In addition to physics, he has degrees in chemistry, philosophy, and psychology. He likes exploring ethical questions through fantasy settings, and enjoys long walks with small dogs. His work has appeared in several magazines, including* Metaphorosis, Hypnos, *and* DreamForge.

An interview with Jacey Bedford

Author of The Amber Crown

Jacey Bedford is the author of seven fast moving, action packed novels, all published by DAW. Her latest, *The Amber Crown*, has just been released and this time the focus is firmly on characters – she's got some great ones here: funny, flawed and relatable, all struggling to deal with their worlds being turned upside down.

Jacey writes science fiction *and* fantasy, which is an unusual but not unique combination. *The Amber Crown* is firmly in the fantasy category, though the fantasy elements are light and grounded. It's a standalone novel, unlike her previous two trilogies, but like the others, it weighs in with a hefty word count. She's understandably enthusiastic: "If I told you *all* about it we'd be here for hours. It's quite a chunky book. Plenty to get your teeth into. It's called *The Amber Crown* and it's due out from DAW on 11th January 2022 in trade-paperback (large) format. It's a standalone historical fantasy set in a country not unlike the Baltic States, in a time period not unlike the mid 1600s. It's about three people caught up in the aftermath of the assassination of King Konstantyn of Zavonia, a good king who might even have been a great king had he had a few more years. My three characters are Valdas, captain of the King's High Guard and responsible for the king's safety. Oops. Mirza is a Landstrider witch who can walk the spirit world, and Lind is the clever assassin who started the whole sorry chain of events in the first place. The King's heir is his older cousin, Gerhard who is a smoky lamp glass to Konstantyn's shining light. Konstantyn once pointed out that Gerhard would be hard pressed to find his arse with his hand without his secretary,

Kazimir. Valdas is accused of the murder, and so he's on the run, but still determined to find the real killer and avenge Konstantyn. The three characters start out separately but come together through the book as a dark power rises in the capital. The country is going to Hell, soon to be fighting a war on two fronts which it cannot win. Can these three set things right?

The Amber Crown feels similar in feel to the *Shadow and Bone* stories by Leigh Bardugo, which are similarly set in a fictionalised Eastern Europe (expertly dramatized in a recent Netflix series. That's a rich backdrop, but it's also potentially constraining, It's not quite *Bridgerton*, but there are more black and minority characters than I would have expected. Here, a (presumably) Romany group becomes renamed 'Landstriders', no doubt so that the unique and historically contentious issues surrounding this group don't dominate the manuscript. I wondered if she'd ever considered making the setting completely fictional. "It was, originally- and it is completely fictional really, it's just got that Baltic flavour. I looked at the actual history of the Baltics, and it's set, in my had, in about 1650, but I don't think I ever mention that but at that time Sweden was running rampant and taking over everything, and there weren't any Kingdoms then, so I originally looked at much earlier – the Northern Crusades, which if you think of crusades you think of.. desert… Jerusalem (but) there were a whole series of crusades into the Baltics and it was actually the last part of Europe to be Christianised… you don't think of the Baltics as the last bastion of paganism, but it actually was.

"Poland in particular was quite cosmopolitan then, so I've taken that aspect and tried to people it with people of different colours and religions. It was quite free at that point."

The three main viewpoint characters - the witch, the assassin and the soldier - are all very different and they all bring unique stories to the table. I wondered if Jacey had a favourite,

"That's a difficult one because I like all three main characters for different reasons. Valdas is very straightforward. What you see is what you get. He's a genuine war hero, but he never makes a big thing out of it. He's resolute and honourable, with a big heart. He likes women… and sex… and when given the opportunity he will rise to the occasion. But he will always take no for an answer. And that bit about liking women… he likes what's in their heads as well as what's between their legs. Mirza has overcome enormous difficulties to become witch-healer of the Landstrider band. She's admired and feared in equal measure for her abilities, her sharp tongue, and the witchmark which stains the side of her face port-wine-red. When the spirit of Valdas's dead king gives her a task she fears it's a journey she might never return from. And then there's Lind, assassin-for-hire with a terrible childhood and more hangups than your average wardrobe. Lind is the character with the biggest journey, so he was fun to write. See, I'm still no closer to discovering which one is my favourite. Please don't make me choose."

Is this a book with a happy ending? Well, her characters "all get what they need; it might not necessarily be what they thought they wanted," For instance, in the early stages it's hard to imagine the fabulously layered and deeply damaged assassin Lind finding any sort of peace, let alone any sympathy from readers, but it's a mark of good writing that we get to see beneath his icy exterior – and appreciate the journey he's on.

In many ways this is classic fantasy, but the novel is surprisingly racy. Jacey chuckled and agreed – sex is an important part of the journeys of her three main characters, For Valdas it's about affirmation, for Mizra it's discovery and for Lind, who has more than a few debilitating mental scars, it's all about healing. So, with the faux history a la *Highlander*, and a very steamy accent to her heroes' interactions, is she the new Diana Gabaldon?

In line with writers like Lois McMaster Bujold, Anne Leckie, George Martin and Elizabeth Moon, Jacey Bedford swaps between fantasy and science fiction. She tells me she enjoys both, so writes both. Her first published novel was her 'Psi-Tech' science fiction novel, *Empire of Dust*, but she wrote her fantasy novel *Winterwood* before that – the vagaries of the publishing schedule meant they came out in reverse order. I asked her if it was hard to prevent fantasy from creeping in to her sci-fi, and vice-versa. And which does she like best?

"I like writing character-driven fiction, so in a way there's not much difference between writing science fiction and fantasy. The writing techniques are the same, it's just the worldbuilding that changes. My science fiction is space opera, or you could even call it science fantasy. I do a lot of handwaving towards the actual science of space travel, and I have humans (or maybe post-humans) enhanced by implants that enable telepathy. It's really all about the characters and the difficulties I throw at them.

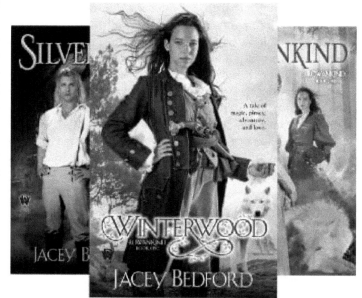

"In my Psi-Tech trilogy (*Empire of Dust; Crossways; Nimbus*) my telepaths take a stand against spacefaring corporations whose gross domestic product is greater than any one planetary government… until aliens in foldspace change the game completely.

"In my fantasy I veer towards the historical. My Rowankind trilogy (*Winterwood; Silverwolf; Rowankind*) is set in 1800, with Napoleon rampaging across Europe, while George III is bonkers (for a good magical reason). My main character is Rossalinde (Ross) Tremayne, a widowed cross-dressing privateer captain accompanied by her crew of barely reformed pirates and the jealous ghost of her late husband. Oh, yes, and she's an unregistered witch, which could get her hanged if the Mysterium catches up with her. There's nothing terribly scientific in the Rowankind books, but I had to do a lot of research about the period, especially about the mechanics of sailing a tops'l schooner..

Jacey was born and brought up in Yorkshire, within spitting distance of current Do Who Jodie Whittaker. As she tells me: "I began riding horses at the age of seven and always wanted to run a riding school, but lack of money sent me off to college (you could get grants in those days) so I started out my working life as a librarian umpty-twiddly years ago. If I couldn't have horses, then books were the next best thing. I married Brian, my long-term boyfriend (a musician and teacher) when I was twenty, and we're still married. Post library, and post two children, we ended up in a vocal trio with a friend, Hilary. In 1989 we kicked our day jobs in the head and went on the road with Artisan for close to twenty years. (www.artisan-harmony.com). We did thousands of ecologically unfriendly road-miles, and thirty-one tours to Canada, the USA and (once) to Australia via Hong Kong. Now I sit behind a desk as a music booking agent, though we never say never again if asked to do the occasional concert. I've always written, though the world will be relieved to know that I never finished my first book, a future dystopia peopled with versions of my favourite pop stars. (Eat your heart out, Hunger Games.) In my defence I was only sixteen.

Jacey is an integral part of the UK sci-fi and fantasy community, and regularly appears on panels at the two main writer-based conference events, science fiction's *Eastercon* and *Fantasycon*. She also acts as the principal organiser for the long-running *Milford* workshop, a high-level critiquing group of established and emerging writers. I asked her about it.

"It's been going since 1956 in the USA and came to England with James Blish in 1972. It's an annual gathering of published SF/F writers who meet to critique each other's work. We're kettled up together for a week (maximum 15 attendees) in a delightful setting in North Wales. It's a social as well as a writing thing."

It rains a lot at Milford and the wi-fi is rubbish, which is a good way of keeping people focused on writing. Do people thrive with that enforced seclusion?

"There are no teachers or students, just other writers whose aim is to improve each piece critted. Over the years many famous writers have passed through: George R.R. Martin, Anne McCaffrey, Brian Aldiss, Chris Priest, Charlie Stross, Alastair

Reynolds. I've been so many times that eventually they gave me a job to do, so I'm currently the secretary. You can read all about it at www.milfordSF.co.uk. I got my first book deal via a recommendation from a fellow author at Milford to her editor at DAW, and since who gets published and who doesn't is often down to luck and persistence, I think Milford helped to change my life!"

Milford is full every year, but every workshop has places open for people who haven't been before and so the collective conversation continues to be enriched by new voices. As workshops go, it's relatively cheap since there are no paid facilitators, but it's residential and costs have to be covered so there are some bursaries available each year for people in underrepresented groups – more details on their website.

There's a Milford retreat once a year too – no critiquing but a week of fine food and good company with plenty of lively conversation in the suitably writer-ly library room. You need some published writing history to be eligible for both retreat and workshop, but the mic of new writers and old hands is one of the things that gives Milford its strength,

Although Jacey's English her publisher, DAW is American and she has an

American agent and editor. I put it to her that must lead to some interesting editorial conversations, and we talked about her tug of war on getting round the very American word 'gotten.' Her books are typeset in American English, which reflects the market where most of her sales are, but she relies on her editor to add Americanisms.

I wondered if working with a US team had influenced the way she writes, and what it's like working with people across continents.

"I can tell you one thing… I use a lot more commas than I used to. Sheesh, I've never seen as many added commas as I found in my very first published book. To me it looked as if the copy-editor had taken a big bucket of commas and dumped it over my manuscript. Commas after fronted adverbials, Oxford commas, you name it, they sprinkled it mightily with commas. I've recovered from my shock now, and I'm conscious of using a lot more commas as I write… but the copy editors still add more.

"The copy editor's job is to smooth out any glitches in prose and punctuation and to check to see if I've made an idiot of myself by changing someone's name in all but one missed chapter. She also changes my British English into American English (though I'll never get used to 'traveler' with one L.) Working across continents is no problem at all. My editor usually phones me up and talks at me for an hour at a time while I scribble notes frantically. Thanks to Worldcons in London, Helsinki and Dublin, World Fantasycon in Brighton, and Eastercon in Harrogate, we've met a number of times. She came to stay with us for a few days, after Harrogate, and I was able to show her some of the real locations that I borrowed for my Rowankind books. I am

profoundly grateful for all the staff at DAW: my editor who does a structural edit, my copy editor, and all the proofreaders who turn my manuscript into something that looks professional. Getting a book out there is a team effort."

Such are the delays inherent in publishing that there have been a couple of years between Jacey sending *The Amber Crown* to her publisher sand it finally appearing in print. But when I asked what was next in the pipeline, Jacey was uncharacteristically vague. "Oooh another difficult question. I have a pair of books that were on a back burner for a while, but I've recently revised them and I think they've got legs. They are set in my Psi-Tech universe, but located on one planet in the far future. I also have a couple of YA novels (unrelated to each other) which are with my agent at the moment. I wasn't very productive, writing-wise, during lockdown. Like other people have said, it seemed as though the world was on hold, and so was my brain, though I did some editing and wrote a short story for 'Derelict,' an anthology published by Zombies Need Brains Press. I do, however have ten thousand words which could turn into the start of a new science fiction book - or should that be science fantasy? Right now I'm busy writing blog posts, and doing interviews to support the release of *The Amber Crown*."

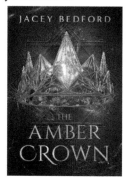

The Amber Crown is available now from DAW worldwide in trade paperback and ebook.

Hear more from Jacey at www.jaceybedford.co.uk, and follow her on Twitter @jaceybedford, facebook.com/Jacey.bedford.writer or sign up for her mailing list at www.jaceybedford.co.uk/contact.htm

The Exquisite Artifacts of Sir Drustan the Bold

Priscila Santa Rosa

The dragon didn't frighten Adelynn, not when it roared, exposing rows of serrated teeth, nor when it hissed, letting smoke escape from under its bright orange scales. What made her hands shake and her gaze fall was the sound of the whip and the high-pitched whine that followed it.

"See, wife? How it cowers with the right amount of strength applied to the strike?" her husband said with a satisfied smile. "Size is irrelevant."

She had never asked him to explain the nuances of torture—if there was such a thing—but Sir Drustan the Bold often assumed he knew the inner workings of her mind better than she did.

"At this rate, I'll be able to fly it to the tournament. No one will deny my deeds then," he continued. "No, I daresay the king will rush to build me a statue."

The dungeon was thick with shadows, its stony walls purposefully devoid of torches, but the animal emanated an unnatural glow that revealed its strange features. Hard scales covered its body and colorful plumage decorated its long spine. It had the face and mane of a lion combined with the body of a snake. It was unlike anything she had ever seen, but then again, she had seen very little of anything at all growing up in the Tower.

"I see no wings," Adelynn finally said.

"What?" Drustan barked. He wiped the blood off the whip, acting as if he had forgotten the sound of her voice. "I don't follow."

"How does it fly?"

He threw a glance at the creature, cocking his head and narrowing his eyes. Then, he waved her off. "Some mysterious

51

magical force, no doubt. What difference does it make? What matters is that I captured it and brought it from exotic lands where none at court dared to venture yet!"

He lifted his hand again, ready to inflict a new injury, but the dragon anticipated his movement. With a hiss, it scurried to the farthest corner of the cage and curled its lengthy body onto itself. Perhaps it was selfish of her, but she felt a pang of disappointment at its recoiling. Fight him, she thought, or perhaps prayed.

"It seems it has learned its lesson well," Drustan said with a smirk. He then rolled the whip and placed it back onto the weapon rack. "All this exercise has made me hungry."

She didn't take her eyes off the dragon. "I already had the cook prepare you lunch."

"Good." He nodded, and then strode out of the dungeon, whistling as he went up the stairs.

Adelynn stayed behind, knowing a meal and the kitchen maid would distract him from her absence. Instead, she stepped toward the cage. Without Drustan's booming voice and the snapping of his whip, the dragon's labored breathing echoed around the walls. It had been fighting off Drustan's lashings and commands for the better part of a month, and its scales were marked by harsh, scabby scars that flared hot red at each breath the creature took.

As she slowly moved closer to the bars, the dragon's bright blue eyes followed her. She avoided looking directly at it, preferring to sneak a glance while keeping her head down. With subtle movements, she reached for her pouch and took out a piece of salted salmon she had taken out of the kitchen. Like she had done countless times to persuade stray cats and tiny mice to keep her company in the Tower, she left the food inside the cage. She made sure to place it far enough so the dragon would sense it as an invitation, not an order. She knew Sir Drustan had the stablehands feeding the dragon only once a week. A starved animal was an animal desperate to please—or so the knight believed.

"I'm sorry," she whispered, head still down. The dragon hissed. "Eat. It'll help."

The hiss turned into a low growl. With a sigh, she knelt near the cage to make herself smaller and less threatening. She sat there for a long time, listening to the dragon's rapid breathing until eventually it slowed down. Only then she risked meeting its gaze. Even half-hidden between the layers of its curled body, the dragon's blue eyes shone in the dark. After a few seconds, it blinked slowly in a small gesture of trust.

"Hello," she whispered. "Hello there."

It let out a long snort. A puff of warm smoke crossed the cage, carrying the aroma of a lit fireplace on a winter night. She smiled.

The day the dragon arrived at Eyrecourt castle, everyone had been on edge, even Drustan. Apparently, it had almost killed a sailor during the sea journey. A considerable amount of coin was spent to arrange for its transportation and eight horses had pulled the chained animal into the gardens. It took a cauldron of potions to numb it enough before it stopped struggling and biting those nearby. This was not a stray cat or a bird seeking a safe perch. But the moment Adelynn had stepped out of Drustan's shadow to look at the dragon up close, something had stirred inside her.

In those large blue irises she had seen her own reflection, but the woman looking back was a stranger; a phantom drifting two steps behind her owner. Through those eyes, she saw a truth she had hidden even from herself.

Her transformation had been slow, and not marked by whipping and starvation. The erosion of Adelynn, the princess living in a tower who dreamt of freedom, happened gradually in the quietness of everyday vile deeds.

To the dragon, the whip. To the wife, a hand over her mouth. Adelynn and the dragon. Both were pieces of the same collection.

"He used to be gentle," she said to the dragon, a heavy weight growing in her chest. "He used to find beauty in the world."

But maybe that was a lie, too.

Their courtship had been full of promises – not unusual, she knew. <u>Your beauty leaves me without words</u>, Drustan had said. What he meant was he had no words to describe love because he knew nothing of it. <u>I'll keep you safe</u>, he had said. He kept her locked away instead.

Perhaps the cruelest lie had been wrapped in a promise. <u>I will show you the world</u>, Drustan had vowed. What he meant was he would show <u>her</u> to the world. Before the wedding ceremony, when longing was confused with desire, he had paraded Adelynn all over the kingdom. They would hop from castle to castle, from palaces to temples. She was dazzled by the attention at first, and then each encounter drained a little more of her. Piece by piece, she gave herself away to be placed on his shelf.

"I suppose that's no comfort to you," she continued. "I suppose it doesn't make a difference."

The dragon lifted its head as if daring her to continue. The feathers covering its body fluttered slightly.

"You didn't say yes. You didn't let him charm you into new, prettier chains." She looked at the ring around her finger. "Maybe a captive bird will always love its cage."

Shaking its orange and purple mane, the dragon unwrapped its body. Then, it lunged. With one rapid strike, it ate the salmon, swallowing it whole. The motion was smooth and precise. Adelynn's smile grew brighter.

"But you're no bird, are you? You're something else entirely. And you don't deserve this place."

To her surprise, the dragon didn't retreat. Its head stayed close to the bars, so close she could extend her hand and touch its feathers.

And so she did. Like a reckless child wanting to test how hot a flame can be, she reached out.

To its credit, it simply hissed and retreated back into the corner, fleeing her touch immediately. A bite might've made her feel better about the realization that she had frightened it. For the poor animal, she might as well have a whip in her hand. The thought made her nauseated. Real trust was built, not snatched at the earliest opportunity. A lesson she never quite grasped, it seemed.

"I'm sorry." She stood and hurried out.

A few sets of stairs later and Adelynn found herself navigating the upper grounds of Eyrecourt Castle. She hoped the lush gardens—with its marble statues of great heroes and reflective ponds— would calm her. But the castle never offered her any comfort before. It would not start now.

By saving her from the tallest tower in the kingdom (had it been the second tallest, he wouldn't have bothered with it), Drustan had earned Eyecourt Castle. The castle was the king's wedding gift for the happy couple, and it was a glorious one. But no matter how many piles of gold Drustan's treasury held or how long his parties lasted, the shine would wear off to reveal the rust below. The fifty bedrooms, all lavishly decorated, were connected by secret passageways that led to Drustan's own room. He had requested that particular architectural feature personally. Her bedroom, the one thing she asked for after two years of marriage, eventually gained other quirks, such as moving eyes in pictures and a broken lock no smithy could fix.

Eyrecourt was indeed beautiful, but, like her, it was hollowed from the inside. It was worse than her childhood prison. She used to think she missed the Tower and its solitude. For a long time, she had blamed that longing, and herself, for her unhappiness.

The Tower was meant to protect her. The tasks needed to unlock her door were a way for a suitor to prove his worth. Drustan had slain monsters, plucked the purest rose from the highest mountain, climbed the Tower and offered the flower to her wearing a beautiful, charming smile. Her dream, which she had no hand in fulfilling, had become reality. Her parents, strangers in gold and silver, were overjoyed. And Sir Drustan the Bold took his prize.

So, if everything had fallen into place, why did she find herself always wandering hallways barefooted to avoid the silk sheets and the four-posted bed waiting for her in the dark? The answer must be her. She was the problem.

But since the dragon's arrival that thought rang false.

Later that day, she sneaked more salmon into its cage but left as quickly as possible.

Drustan's taming attempts continued, and so did his liberal use of the whip. He eventually felt confident enough to bring the dragon to the gardens. The violent spectacle now happened in full view of the staff. At first, cooks, maids and gardeners were fascinated by the animal, stopping their work to watch the knight perform his circus act. Wonder eventually turned into silence as Drustan's broad smile and wide-eyed joy became a little too intense.

Adelynn felt embarrassed and ashamed of his displays. She wished she could say she had been horrified as well, but familiarity stripped away that part of her too.

One dark afternoon, she placed a hand on his arm, trying to lower the whip in his hand. Any other day, she would've never dared such act, but she couldn't stand others witnessing her private fears.

"That's enough, husband," she whispered. When he turned and brushed off her hand away, she added, "People are watching."

Sweat ran freely on his face. His hair, so carefully brushed and maintained, was disheveled. The mask he only abandoned in the darkness of the bedroom or in the absence of prying eyes had slipped completely. And she was the one feeling exposed.

"Drustan," she said. "Please."

His glare finally left her. He scanned their surroundings, perhaps finally noticing what she had been keenly aware of all along: horrified expressions, hands over mouths, and even a few tears from the people who had admired Sir Drustan the Bold all their lives.

"It's just an animal," he said, quietly at first. Then, he adjusted himself and lowered the whip. He cleared his throat. Loudly, he pronounced, "I have no choice. This is how you tame such a beast."

Furtive glances were exchanged. Some even dared to whisper. Drustan's expression darkened.

"I have a duty to tame this creature," he said, turning to the crowd. "To ensure it will never turn against us. Without me, it would tear your limbs and eat your flesh. I am your protector! You must trust I know what's best."

She bit her lip. His speech was doing little to assuage fears. His threats also rang hollow when the supposedly fierce dragon lay curled onto itself, bleeding and huffing in pain.

A cook shook his head. A young housemaid hid her face behind a friend.

Drustan laughed. "You dare to judge me? Me? I'll prove to all of you. I will ride this beast."

Adelynn reached for his arm. "Perhaps we should retire for the evening, Drustan."

Between gritted teeth, he said, "Shut your mouth."

He whistled for the stablehands. With some hesitation, the men pulled the dragon's chains, forcing it to spread its body. A special saddle was fastened on its back, behind the mane.

The knight pushed her out of the way, and with a broad smile, marched toward the dragon. The creature tried to scurry back, but the whip and the heavy chains forced it to accept as Drustan climbed onto its body and sat on the saddle. At his signal, the men released the chains and dashed out of the way.

The dragon remained still, eyes half-closed. For half-a-second, it seemed like it would do nothing, but then Drustan snapped the whip in the air and the sound was enough. The dragon bolted forward with a roar. Adelynn was thrown in the air, landing in a water pond nearby. When she got up, soaking wet, she could only gasp as the dragon made a sharp turn and flung itself against the walls of the castle.

Drustan jumped off before being squashed between the wall and the dragon's body. He rolled on the ground, bracing himself with grace. Meanwhile, the dragon turned again, eyes set on the knight. It used the wall to propel itself even faster. With its mouth wide open, it lunged.

Adelynn hopped out of the pond and ran.

Just as the dragon's jaws closed, Drustan leaped out of the way. While the dragon recovered from hitting the ground, he found his footing and dashed toward the discarded whip.

But Adelynn was faster. She picked the weapon and stared at it.

"Throw it!" Drustan yelled with a hand extended in her direction. "Give it to me! Quickly!"

She raised her head. Behind her husband, the open mouth of the dragon grew bigger and bigger. Drustan followed her widened gaze. He turned his head, and then dived to the side. The abyss was now coming for her.

She closed her eyes and fell to her knees. She heard screams. Then something warmed her cheeks and the smell of burning pine overwhelmed her senses. Slowly, carefully, she opened her eyes.

The dragon looked at her. She looked at the dragon. It let out a snort, and the smoke watered her eyes. Heart beating loudly in her ears, she stood. The whip fell from her hand.

In the background, she heard wails of pain, but everything else was distant, foggy. She started raising her hand, but then hesitated. The dragon moved closer, letting its mane brush her fingers.

"Shoot it!" someone yelled.

The mane was soft and warm on her skin. She was about to caress it when the dragon let out a high-pitched whine and its eyes rolled to the back of his head. It fell on the ground, unconscious.

Someone yanked her back. As the stablehand dragged her away from the scene, she saw Drustan wriggling in pain on the ground, hand over a mangled, bloodied foot. Three others surrounded the knight, trying to help him but being yelled at to stay away. The dragon had been shot with multiple crossbow bolts and a green substance dripped from them.

In the end, the dragon had stayed firmly on the ground. Drustan's pride was wounded, but an injured foot confined him to a bed. There, his wrath manifested itself with shouting and fits of anger, as bowls of food and cups of medicine were thrown over housemaids' heads.

"How long until he recovers?" Adelynn asked the healer. She had waited for him in the hallway, not eager to enter the lion's den.

"The bite was deep, but he's a strapping young lad and recovery is likely. I gave him a potion for the pain and scarring. As long as he follows my instructions, he'll recover soon."

Her smile felt painful. "Wonderful news."

"Wife!" Drustan barked from the bedroom. "Here. Now!"

The healer apparently didn't notice the anger in Drustan's voice. He patted Adelynn's hand and promptly left.

With her hands closed into fists, she stepped into the bedroom. A dozen incense burners filled the room with fragrant smoke, but even they could not completely hide the pungent odor of sweat and pus. Slightly nauseated, she stood by the door. Drustan was resting above the sheets with only a towel covering his midriff. His body glistened with sweat. Her eyes were drawn to his injured foot. It was blackened, mangled, and oozing fluid.

"I'm hot. I'm in pain. I'm bloody furious, and you disappear for the entire day!" he yelled. "Where were you?"

"I—"

"I want the incense gone! It gives me a headache. I expect a cold bath twice a day. And the bandages must be cleaned three times. The wound will fester otherwise."

"I'll tell the housemaids that—"

He pointed his finger at her. "You do it. I want you."

She swallowed dry. "I have other duties—"

"Come here!" She flinched. "Now!"

It took everything in her, but she didn't move. Drustan stared, an incredulous expression on his scratched face.

"You." He shook his index finger. "You wanted me dead. You did it on purpose."

She shook her head. "No—"

"You incited the crowd. You made me look weak." He let out a short, vicious laugh. "I saved your life! I made you. This is how you repay me. With betrayal."

She said nothing. Words wouldn't matter; he would twist them until they fit the palm of his hand. And then he would use it to strike her.

"I want that dragon's head. I want its body chopped into pieces and its feathers plucked for a winter coat."

She breathed in and out. "What about the tournament? You can still fly it. You want to impress the king."

"Are you an idiot? It has no wings. Ergo, it clearly cannot fly. The merchant lied to me."

"Merchant? You bought it? You didn't actually capture it...?"

"It cost me a fortune! A fortune I amassed performing brave deeds. What matters if I didn't hunt it myself?" He rolled his eyes. "You know nothing of bravery."

At her silence, he glared at her. She managed to return his gaze for a few seconds, but eventually looked down at her feet.

"You're so hard to love," he finally said. "I crave you, yet you reject me at every turn. I, the man who saved you. I gave you a castle. I shower you with gifts. I beg for your love, but you turn away from my touch every night. Now, you want me dead."

"I don't. I..."

"Then, give me the head of the dragon. It has injured your lover, your savior. Don't you want justice for me? Don't I deserve it?"

"Why me? Why can't you do it?"

"I proved my love when I climbed that tower. My hands were bleeding by the end, you know. I almost fell, but I never gave up. Ordering the death of an animal pales in comparison."

She furrowed her brow, the memory of their first meeting transforming into the memory of his first lie. "I..."

"I can't take rejection anymore. You'll force me to do something drastic if you refuse this."

She stared at the floor, muttering, "I'll do as you say."

"I didn't hear you. Speak up!"

She opened her mouth but found it painful to repeat the words. She would not kill the dragon. It... No. He wasn't a mindless monster, but an innocent creature. Adelynn had no one to seek for help, but the dragon had her. She couldn't just stand and watch anymore.

She closed her eyes and took a deep breath. Finally, she raised her head, and perhaps for the first time in her life, Adelynn lied not out of fear, not out of avoidance or supplication. She looked at Drustan's eyes and lied with righteous purpose. "I'll do as you say, husband."

"I knew you would," he said.

But his voice barely registered. Her mind was already racing. If the dragon couldn't fly and there was no sneaking an animal of that size out of the castle, how could she free it? It was Drustan himself who gave her a solution, although she doubted he had noticed his slip.

Adelynn marched to the treasury, where the knight kept his collection of magical artifacts. If the dragon couldn't fly, she would <u>make</u> him fly.

She ignored the flashy treasure, the oil paintings, the golden statues and marble busts. She passed by the ornate weapons and stuffed animal heads. In the back, where torchlight almost couldn't reach, she found Drustan's old gear. He had bragged once about killing a traveling apothecary who wrote a rare book of magical potions. He gave no reason for the murder except that it involved her, but the way he described climbing her tower had jolted her memory.

After all, how could she forget the way Sir Drustan the Bold opened her door, strode inside, and held a white rose to her? She had memorized the gesture for so long; there was no way she was mistaken. His hands were not bloodied. In fact, he didn't have a single strand of hair out of place. He had been magical in every way. Too magical.

She threw things around, yanked drawers, and kicked chests open. Eventually, she found the book.

She spent the next few days preparing a cauldron worth of potion. Every night, she would give the dragon a dose with his salmon. To Drustan, she justified the little side project as a way to keep the animal asleep until the royal executioner's arrival. That lie might not have worked if Drustan hadn't decided threatening servants and refusing to drink his medicine was more important than paying attention to her words.

The night before the executioner's arrival, Adelynn visited the dragon one last time. As she got closer to the bars, he quickly slithered toward her. After making sure no one was watching, she unlocked the cage and stepped inside.

"How are you, boy?" she whispered, patting his snout and letting his mane wrap around her. The dragon purred. "Tonight is the night. Are you ready?"

She threw a salmon on the ground and watched as it was quickly swallowed whole. Then, she threw another, but this time outside the cage. The dragon stared at the fish, but made no move to eat it.

"Go on now."

She had to step out herself before the dragon risked following her. She couldn't blame him—the cage, for all its terrors, was familiar now.

She soaked the last salmon with the potion. If she had done her math correctly, and if the peddler hadn't lied, that would be the last dose.

"I don't know how long this will last, so you might not be able to go back home. But even if you can't, you'll be free," she said, feeling something stuck in her throat. "If you go south, you'll find the sea. There's plenty of fish there. Just... don't eat cattle. They might hunt you for that."

The dragon snorted, eyes fixed on her. He was waiting for the salmon. She smiled. Of course he was.

"Here."

One gulp later and the air changed. The dragon's feathers fluttered. She blinked, and then a burst of wind took the air out of her lungs. The dragon hovered above her, twirling in the air as if dancing. He flew up and up, until he became a tiny silhouette against the full moon.

For a moment, she thought he was gone. Her eyes stung a bit. Then, the dragon dropped down and swept past her, freeing her hair out of its ponytail. She let out a joyful laugh as he landed and nudged her carefully with its head.

"It's okay. Go." She brushed his mane. "I'll find you. Soon."

He purred one last time, and then launched himself back in the air, quickly going over the castle walls. She watched his form become smaller and smaller, then

finally disappear. Afterward, she let her gaze linger on the stars and the moon.

For a long time, she stood there with a pang in her chest she couldn't quite understand. But, whatever emotions bubbled inside her, she was keenly aware of her body, of her breathing, her cheeks, of her hands and heart. The night breeze was gentle on her skin, and the aroma of the nearby flowers was suddenly sweet.

As she walked to her bedroom, the hollow halls appeared grandiose instead of empty—the chandeliers, the large windows with stained glass heroes, the white marble floors. Lying on her bed, she raised her hands, staring at her fingers as if they held something akin to magical proprieties. She closed them into fists, and then opened them again. She did this until she was sure the sensation wasn't a trick.

Those hands had freed a dragon. She had freed a dragon. She caught herself sometimes smiling, other times grimacing. Was her heart racing out of joy or utter fear?

The next day, those feelings hadn't scurried back into the dark corners of her mind. As soon as sunlight peeked between curtains, Adelynn got dressed and opened her window to a view of the gardens. The dragon's cage was open. Adelynn waited.

The first stablehand stared at the cage for a few seconds, possibly frozen. A second one appeared, and after throwing his hands in the air, he started shouting at the first. They argued for a few minutes, perhaps trying to escape the task of letting Drustan know of the escape. Finally, one of them dragged his feet toward the castle.

Adelynn turned around and left her bedroom. The stablehand's steps echoed on the hallways while she made her way toward her husband's room. The poor man arrived at Drustan's door just as she did. He glanced at her, face pale with fear. Adelynn nodded.

They both went in. Without the layer of incense, the odor of Drustan's injury and sweat contaminated the entire room. The air was thick with it. Despite the healer's assurances of a speedy recovery, pus kept oozing from the dragon bite. Even now, while he was supposed to be dozing off to a sleeping potion, Drustan was squirming on the bed, a hand covering his face.

"What?" he shouted. "What is it now?"

The stablehand hesitated for a second before daring to step further into the room. "Sir Drustan, the dragon..."

"Has the royal executioner finally arrived?"

"He will this afternoon," Adelynn said.

"Good!"

"N-no, my lord... Not good," the poor servant continued. "The dragon has... Somehow, the cage was left open, although I have no idea how, and I can't understand it, but..."

"Out with it already!"

After his Adam's apple fell and rose, the stablehand delivered the inevitable news. "The dragon escaped during the night. It's gone, my lord."

Silence fell— a sharp silence, the kind that felt accompanied by a blade near a neck. Drustan lowered his hand to finally look at them in the eye. Adelynn had to remind herself that he could not reach her in his condition, not if she stayed by the doorway.

"Very well. I'm glad," he whispered, then continued with a high-pitched tone. "I'm relieved to be rid of the beast no matter how! Yes. Indeed! Good riddance!"

Relief was plainly written on the stablehand's face. He closed his eyes and let out a sigh. Adelynn remained still.

"However," Drustan added. "However... This cannot go unpunished. The dragon was my property and you, you imbecile, have lost it."

"My lord—"

"—No one speaks of this outside these walls, or you'll lose your position... and your head. Understood?"

The man fell on his knees and nodded his head desperately. "Yes! Of course! Thank you, my lord."

"Run along now. I have business with my dear wife."

While the man scurried away, Adelynn and Drustan stared at each other. This time she noticed his ashen appearance—the dark circles under his eyes, the glistening sweat running from his hairline to his jaw, the stubble not yet trimmed. Even as they battled silently, he couldn't help but flinch at the pain he no doubt was feeling. He used to tower over her, to corner her, to trap her, and she had always fled his eyes. Perhaps his petrifying spell was broken by her gaze.

"So, you freed the beast."

"I did."

His laugh was hollow and shallow, bitter cold. "Not even an attempt at an excuse. How daring. I suppose you're also poisoning me. Finishing the job the dragon started."

She shook her head. "I would never do such a thing."

He pointed at his injury. It was swollen, redden and oozing cloudy pus. "What's this then?"

"I don't know. I'm not a healer."

"You do know! You do know because this is your doing! You've planned this since the start. You forced me to ride that creature! And now, you freed it just as the royal executioner arrives, just in time for him to witness my humiliation. No doubt the healer has been bribed to ignore my plight."

Adelynn blinked. Her husband seemed smaller now that fear had left her. She searched her heart and found no pity, but also no joy in his situation.

"Your plight isn't ignored. Your injury has worsened because you refuse to listen to the healer. You have repeatedly thrown potions at the poor maids, refusing to drink them if they are too hot or too cold. You snap and yell at anyone trying to change your bandages. You've allowed your wound to become a matter of pride. And no healer can cure pride."

For once, Drustan had no words. He opened and closed his mouth, nostrils flaring.

"I'll tell the royal executioner that the dragon tried to escape and was killed before he could hurt anyone. The matter will be forgotten eventually," she continued, neglecting to explain her motivation was purely to keep attention off the dragon. "Once you recover—"

"Once I recover, I will make sure you pay for this."

"I won't be here for that. I'm leaving."

"You have nowhere to go! Your parents are dead. The king will not believe you over me. And you won't survive out there without my protection."

"I don't want to survive. I want to have a life, a dream, a hope. And you... you have stolen too many years of my life already."

He almost fell from the bed trying to reach her, but his injury was too painful. Instead, he threw insult after insult as she turned around and left.

After weeks of traveling, of following sightings of a strange beast, they finally found each other again. Eventually, the dragon lowered his head and waited for her. The first time she held his mane and the ground disappeared from under them, Adelynn thought she was about to die. Then, it was the only way for her to feel alive.

She chose her old tower as their home. Bandits couldn't climb it, and wild beasts wouldn't come near it. It was quiet and reclusive, but not a prison nor a cage. Not anymore.

If she wanted to leave, all she needed to do was whistle and the dragon would come. The potion had never worn off. Perhaps it was a miracle. Perhaps the dragon had always been able to fly. She didn't understand, and it didn't matter.

They often went to the sea, where he would fly near the water, close enough for her to wet her toes as he snapped up fish. They challenged their lungs going above the clouds, hoping to see where the sky and the heavens met. Sometimes, they stayed firmly on the ground, with Adelynn reading a book while resting her back against his mane.

From traveling traders, she heard stories of a knight dying after a terrible beast attacked him. She heard how his castle was given away to some other brave warrior and how the exquisite artifacts in his collection were auctioned to merchants all over the kingdom. The absence of his wife was never mentioned. But she had never existed, not really.

Instead, Adelynn preferred the stories of a woman riding a beautiful dragon, visiting distant lands and going on mysterious adventures. Those stories she had made real.

Priscila Santa Rosa is a Brazilian writer, a voracious reader, and an amateur baker. In a past life, she was a graphic designer, and in an imagined future she's spectacularly wealthy, yet artistically uncompromised. Her work has been published in Dime Show Review and Scarlet Leaf Review. She was born in São Paulo, Brazil at a time when shoulder pads were still a thing and during the terrible age of the mullet.

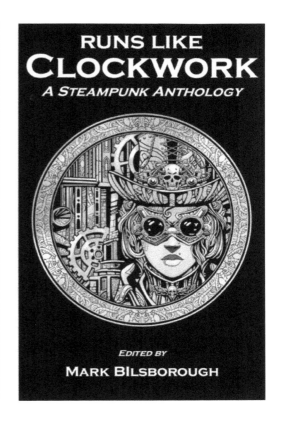

There's No Barking on Mars

Russell Weisfield

I hated my parents for wanting me to leave Olympus behind on Earth. Who tells a little girl that the puppy Santa brought her two Christmases before needs to stay while she moves to Mars? Obviously, people who know about space radiation, animal psychology, and similar things which, thirty years ago, meant nothing to me. All I knew was I had spent a Friday night agonizing over what to bring to Mars before piling it in our family den. My parents were then removing all of Olympus's stuff that I had lugged out.

"No, Riley," my father said. "Olympus can't come with us. She's going to move in with Harper's family."

"But Santa gived Olympus to me, not snotty Harper. It's not fair!" I said.

Olympus agreed by barking at my mother as she hauled away the dog carrier. Admittedly, Olympus was some kind of Yorkie mix, and barked at everything.

"I know it seems unfair," my father said, "but, um, listen to her. She's barking. There's no barking on Mars. It's forbidden."

"Then I'll teach her not to bark."

"Well. . . um. . . it's still very expensive to shuttle Olympus to Mars. Mommy and daddy don't have that much money -- not even with our promotions."

"You can use my allowance."

"Awww, that's sweet of you, kiddo, but. . . still. . . you see. . . " my father turned towards my mother and clasped his hands in prayer.

"Sweetie, do you remember how we'll need spacesuits so we're protected from the harsh Martian environment?" my mother asked.

"Yeah."

"Well, there aren't any spacesuits for dogs."

"Why not? What's so special about spacesuits anyway?"

"Wait here." My mother walked out of the den and returned with my astronaut costume and one of my tee shirts. She guided my hand over each.

"This fabric on the spacesuit is just like the real thing. It's thicker and firmer than your other clothes. When you wear it, it's also tighter."

"Oh, you're right." The fact they had found the mass-produced costume at a garage sale utterly escaped me.

"Do you also remember how we said that we're going to eat strange special food?" I nodded. "Well there isn't any special dog food."

"Why not?"

"Because," she said, "dogs need to eat dog plants and dog plants don't grow on Mars. Only human plants grow there."

My parents conjured up similar answers for my other questions. One was even the old chestnut about my eyes popping out of my head. To my young mind, those answers made sense.

Nonetheless, a million ideas hit me for ways to bring Olympus to Mars. I put them aside the moment Olympus stood by me with a rope toy in her mouth and her tail swishing excitedly. I grinned. This signaled the start of our night routine.

I grabbed the rope and pulled. She chomped down and clenched her jaw. A brief tug of war ensued in which neither of us let go. Eventually, I turned around and pulled. She kept pace as I dragged her all around the house. The game ended when she growled and I released the rope. She then dashed off in triumph with me close behind. The next game had begun.

A few more laps around the house left me tired and sweaty. I collapsed. "I'm tired because I runned too much, Olympus, and both my foots hurt. Stretch time." Saying "stretch time", which my dad said after his mega workouts, caused Olympus to trot over, leap on me, and lick my face. She continued licking until my giggles turned into roaring laughter. "OK, Olympus. Off."

We finished our ritual by finding the red star in the sky. "Look, our new home," I said to a panting Olympus. As soon as I uttered the words, tears welled in my eyes. She wasn't going there.

For the rest of the night, I focused on getting Olympus to Mars. I crossed my heart and vowed that either Olympus would join us, or I would stay. "They can't make me go to Mars," I repeated until I fell asleep.

The next day, I pretended my pickup truck filled with dolls was a spaceship. I flew it around my room before landing it.

"This is captain mommy," I said in an attempt at an authoritative voice. "We've reached the Martian crater. Everybody out. That means you too, Olympus." One by one I took the dolls out of the truck and voiced various greetings such as, "Hello, Mars. Thank you for having us. This is amazing." For the stuffed dog I said, "Yip, yip."

Unbeknownst to me, the real Olympus had entered my room. I shrieked and twirled about when she nosed me in the behind. In response, she ran around with her tail down. While she was running, her left fore paw got caught in one of the dolls' dresses that were strewn about the floor. She nipped at it frantically.

When I finally caught and hugged her, she began to calm. This let me jiggle and maneuver the tightly wrapped dress from around her toes and claws. With a final giant yank, Olympus was free. I sighed.

"Boy, was that ever tight on you."

The moment the words left my mouth, a thought occurred to me. I raced about to feel each of my doll's clothes. I would rub one, shake my head, and move to the next. After the last one, I sat and pouted. Then, I remembered something.

"Daddy, daddy," I shouted. A moment later my dutiful dad stood in the doorway demanding to know the problem. "Are we taking great grandma's dolls with us?"

"No."

"Can I play with them, then? Please?" I batted my eyes and pleaded with a happy smile.

He never let me play with them. The only time I had even seen them was when he sealed them away after telling me great grandma had "gone to the sky."

"I suppose," he said with a sigh. "Just as well, they need to be recalled from the vault, anyway."

Dad briefly conversed with our digital assistant and soon, the whir of an approaching cargo drone sounded through my open window. Dad went outside and returned carrying a wooden box with a velvet lid. Inside were a bunch of antique dolls. They wore clothes filled with polka dots and other old-fashioned or luxurious designs. My smile broadened as I touched each of the thick and firm fabrics. These could be used for a spacesuit!

"Now be careful with them," he said. "They're not quite priceless, but are worth a bit."

"OK," I said. Then, I thought, *If they costed between nothing and a small amount, what's the big deal?*

I stripped off the dresses and casually tossed them in a pile. The dolls I handled more carefully, having concluded they themselves were important and not what they were wearing. For each one, I gingerly carried it to my dresser, wiped away any dust, and slowly set the doll down.

Once all the clothes lay in a pile, I began cutting them up. For accurate measurements, I held the ripped pieces next to Olympus. She barked and licked my face.

"No, Olympus. Sit."

Olympus obeyed, but continued to bark and wag her tail. I cut, trimmed, and glued most of the clothes.

"Roll over, Olympus," I said.

Again, Olympus obeyed. I pulled some torn clothes over each of Olympus's legs. She kicked her legs and squirmed. When I finished, she rolled over and nipped at the clothes that were tied around her legs.

While she did that, I grabbed the biggest piece of clothing in the pile and pulled it over her. Olympus fought to keep the garb off her. At one point, she beelined for the door, but I slammed it shut.

Eventually, that piece of clothing was over her body and tucked into the leggings. To finish off the spacesuit, I needed a helmet like the one for my costume. My goldfish bowl seemed perfect.

Originally, I hoped to give it to great grandma since I was told she was now caring for my goldfish. I figured we might visit her as we shot through the sky on our way off Earth. Therefore, I had included it amongst our items in the den, but my parents forced me to toss it in our thrift store box.

I closed Olympus in my room and ran to retrieve it. Upon returning, I set a tense Olympus on my lap. She tried escaping as I squeezed her head into the bowl. She shook her head and pushed against the glass with her hind paw. The bowl stayed put. Her ensuing barks echoed in a muffled manner.

"Mom, dad, come look what I maked," They hurried into the room. "It's a spacesuit for Olympus!" I jumped up and down beaming with a huge smile while pointing at that hobo looking outfit. My father burst into laughter, but quieted when my gaze fell upon him. "Quick, take a picture and send it to the astronaut captain, so they'll let us take Olympus to Mars."

My mother obligingly snapped a picture. "I'm sending it now."

"When do you think we'll hear back? Soon, I hope."

"Sweetie, we may not hear back at all. Even if we do, we'll still have to find food she can eat. Remember, dog plants don't grow on Mars. We should really plan to leave her with Harper's family."

"Wait, are those the dresses from great grandma's dolls?" my father asked. "Weren't you supposed to be careful with them?"

"Uh huh. That's why I placed the dolls extra careful on the dresser. See." I pointed at the dressers. My father palmed his forehead.

"Honey, those were very valuable. I had planned to sell them."

"Can't you still sell them?"

"Yes, but no one will buy them without the dresses."

"I will. You can take that out of my allowance too." The meager amount seemed infinite to me.

Through gritted teeth, my father slowly said, "I don't think you'll have an allowance after paying for them."

"That's OK. I'll have Olympus."

In the same tone, he said, "I don't think your allowance will pay for both her voyage and the dolls."

"Well, I'll find a way to earn the money. We don't need to give her to Harper." I yelled.

"Easy, Riley," my mother said as she rushed to stand between my father and me. "You know, you've spent the day cooped up in here. Why don't you go play outside?"

"Fine." I trudged off to ride my bike.

Nearby were some woods where the local kids met for games such as kick the can. Within the woods was what we kids called "the secret huge fort." In truth, the fort was neither. It consisted of a few plywood platforms nailed to a pair of low hanging branches on a giant oak tree and some debris for walls. Multiple parents had breached those walls to discover their wayward children hunkering down in a futile attempt to avoid chores or such things. I often went there for the quiet.

After parking my bike at the base of the tree, I climbed up and laid down. I wondered, *Why aren't mom and dad more excited about the spacesuit? And why are they still ready to hand Olympus to Harper? What has she done to deserve a dog? Nothing. Someone even told me Santa placed Harper on his naughty list.*

I spent the rest of the afternoon consumed with stopping Harper from getting Olympus. She lived on the edge of the woods and I stopped there on my way home to glare. Their rubber trash can sat on the curb for the next day's collection. With a solid kick, I knocked it over. Someone across the street hollered at me, but I sped away.

For dinner, my mother decided we should try one of the prepared meals we'd be eating during our voyage. This stuff was nasty! It tasted like Brussels sprouts, peppered steak, buttermilk, and coleslaw all rolled into one. I would scrunch my face and spit out each one of those foods if given to me separately. I wouldn't sample a dish that disgusting again until I ate haggis.

Multiple times I requested something else. Each time my parents refused. By the time they had finished their food and started cleaning the dishes, I still sat with a mostly full plate. When they weren't looking, I shared some with Olympus.

She downed it in seconds and sat with a grateful expression and the politeness she could muster when wanting something. I fed her more. She gobbled down every morsel. She also licked my plate clean. As she did, a smile crept across my face.

If she can eat this, I thought, *then she won't need those dog plants that don't grow on Mars!*

I attempted to tell my parents. They, however, were busy and didn't respond.

Later, after she finished walking Olympus, mom stormed into my bedroom and interrupted dad reading me *Mickey Goes to* Mars. "Riley, what did you feed Olympus?" Her glare pained like being spanked.

"Just her normal food."

"Are you sure you didn't feed her something else?" Her glare intensified.

"Fine. I gave her my space food. But, she really liked it. Don't that mean she can eat human food?"

My mother's expression softened a lot. She wiped her eyes and then stared at my father with her mouth agape.

"Well, you know, uh, just because she can eat human food, doesn't mean she should," my father said. "It might make her very sick. Out of caution, we should probably leave her with the vet until she's healthy. Sadly, she may not be healthy until after we launch for Mars."

"Yeah. Yeah, I'm afraid Daddy's right, sweetie."

I started to panic. My stomach churned. "But mommy, maybe she'll get better first."

"Maybe you're right. Tell you what. I'll take her to the vet after dropping you off at school, and we'll see what the vet says."

"OK," I said as I pouted.

My dad finished reading the story, but I paid no attention. Instead, I brainstormed for ways to get Olympus to Mars. When dad left, I stared out my window at the red star and said, "I hate you". Same as the previous night, I fell asleep repeating, "they can't make me go to Mars."

At school, I sought out Harper. "Why do you get Olympus?"

"What are you talking about?"

"My parents said you're getting my dog."

"We're not getting your old dog. We're getting a puppy dog."

"No, you're not. You're getting Olympus. And you can't have her!"

"Well, I don't want your dog. I want my own dog who won't be named something stupid like Olympus."

I gnashed my teeth. "It's not a stupid name. Do you know why me and my mom choosed that name?"

"No, and I don't care. We're getting a puppy dog tonight from the vet and not naming it Olympus!"

"No you're not! You're lying!" I stuck out both arms and shoved her to the concrete. She cried out. Hooting and cheering erupted nearby. A teacher rushed over, pulled me away, and hauled me to the correction office where they forced me to sit quietly.

This let me think, *Is Harper actually getting a dog from the vet tonight? Is it Olympus? Why would it be Olympus? If she's OK after eating the space food, why isn't she coming home to us?*

My father came and spent a long time talking with the officers and the principal. Afterward, my father took me home. During the ride, he explained that since we were moving soon, he had withdrawn me from school.

The impact of being withdrawn didn't register. Olympus was my only focus. My father, however, refused to answer any questions about her without mom. The whole ride home, I tapped my fingers and gritted my teeth.

As soon as the three of us were together, I blurted out, "Olympus. Where is she?" They didn't even bother with a phony answer.

"Daddy and I thought it would be easiest if we allowed Harper and her family to adopt Olympus now rather than later. I'm sorry, sweetie."

"It's not fair!" I stamped my feet, shook violently, and started to pound my fists on the table. "Up yours, you retards!" I didn't even know what retards meant. Normally, such an outburst would have elicited a severe punishment. This time, my parents only gave pitiful expressions as I stomped to my room.

What was I going to do now? How could my parents shuffle Olympus off, especially without letting me say goodbye? I needed to get Olympus from Harper's family. Then, I could go to the space shuttle with her spacesuit and pay for her voyage with my allowance. Of course, we hadn't heard back from the shuttle captain, so I couldn't be sure they'd let me bring her. I also hadn't paid for the dolls. If what my dad had said was true, then I wouldn't be able to pay for the dolls and for Olympus's trip. At that point, Olympus would be forced to stay on Earth.

Considering everything, the better idea appeared to be just stay on Earth with her. I had repeated that they couldn't make me go to Mars many times. Now, I would prove it.

After getting Olympus, we would need a place to stay. The fort immediately sprang to mind. That place seemed perfect. The more I thought about this, the more I bounced about the room with excitement. It never occurred to me what the consequences might be for stealing Olympus from Harper's. She was my dog, and I intended to get her back.

When my parents had gone to bed, I tiptoed out of my room. Quietly, I stuffed my backpack with my sleeping bag, a flashlight, and supplies for Olympus and myself. The lopsided backpack bit into my shoulder and banged against me as I ran to Harper's.

A plan to spring Olympus, however, remained elusive by the time I arrived. Ringing the doorbell seemed pointless.

Creeping in through a front window also struck me as dumb. The only other idea that occurred to me was to sneak in through the back. I approached the gate to the backyard. My heart pounded against my chest. My breathing quickened.

I pulled on the ancient gate, unsure if it would be locked or begin creaking and wake the family. It opened, and silently, though a scream almost escaped my mouth when a splinter pierced my thumb. Lucky for me, the pain quickly subsided.

I crept along the back of the house. At every window, I ducked. Upon passing the third window, my backpack slid a little off my shoulder and clunked into the house. Barking sounded from inside. I froze. A dark form darted out of a flap at the bottom of the backdoor. It jumped on me and knocked me to the grass.

For the second time that night I almost screamed, but Olympus stifled any such noise by licking me fervently. When she stopped, I leashed her and led her out of the yard.

We trekked to the fort slowly. Unlike when we walked with mom, Olympus sniffed everything. Every hooting owl, rustling leaf, or snapping twig caused her to stop, tense, and bark. Each time she barked, I scolded her and tried pulling her along. She just ignored me. The hair on my arm stood on end the longer we stood still. The scary ordeal took forever.

Reaching the fort caused me to let out a huge sigh. A bunch of time passed while I struggled to haul a reluctant Olympus and our gear up the tree. Exhaustion weighed on me. Somehow, I spread out my sleeping bag, snuggled into it, and zipped it closed. The moment I did, Olympus whined.

"What do you want girl? Are you hungry?" I opened a sandwich bag full of stale kibble.

After lapping it all up, she sat expectantly. I stared back. Her food was all gone and I foolishly hadn't brought more. My rumbling stomach reminded me I also hadn't brought enough for myself. She barked.

"What? What do you want?" She responded by nipping my heels. "Ow!" She never acted like this. What was the problem? Nothing appeased her. Too tired to deal with figuring out why she barked and whined, I simply pulled my sleeping bag over my ears.

A short time later, a foul stench drifted towards me. I opened my eyes and turned on my flashlight. Olympus squatted a few feet away from me.

"Oh, Olympus," I said in an annoyed tone. I searched for something to clean up her droppings. The best option appeared to be her empty bag of kibble. This proved to be less than ideal. While it served its purpose, it didn't mask the smell. It also didn't prevent me from dirtying my hand.

I washed my hand with my remaining water and tossed the no longer empty bag over the side. The smell from the bag quickly dissipated, but a new one lingered. Underneath Olympus, a rather large puddle formed. My sleeping bag lay downslope from Olympus. Unfortunately, I moved too slowly to keep it completely dry,

I shook my index finger at Olympus. "Bad girl." She merely prostrated herself in the corner. I sighed and curled myself into a ball in the dry part of my sleeping bag. Despite my tiredness, sleep eluded me. I tossed and twisted on the warped wood. Finally, I fell asleep searching for the red star.

Cold drizzling rain woke me in the middle of the night. Thunder boomed in the distance. I sat up and trembled -- thunder scared me. Olympus jumped and nudged up next to me. The drizzle had started to soak her coat, causing me to turn my nose at her wet dog odor.

The rain intensified and the tree's canopy provided little shelter. I considered climbing down and searching for another tree, but my muscles ached and the slipperiness of the top rung of the ladder scared me. Instead, I huddled in a corner.

My teeth chattered. My body shivered. The growl of my stomach was drowned out by the approaching storm and its scary thunder. Each tear that flowed out of my eyes cut across my face in a path distinct from the raindrops.

"I wish mommy was here." Olympus picked up the rope toy that had been dumped out of my backpack and wagged her tail. "Oh stop it. If not for you, I'd be in my nice, soft, warm bed. I also wouldn't be hungry."

"And, my poor heel wouldn't hurt because you bitted me. And, I wouldn't be wet or reek like your poop. So don't think I'm playing with you tonight."

Sometime after dawn, the rain stopped. By that time, I was unable to cry any more. My lips were chapped and cracked, my clothes were drenched, and my breath came in short and shallow bursts. Any movement caused my muscles to scream.

An eternity passed before rustling tree branches and approaching footsteps sounded. Another eon ticked away until my mother peered into the fort with panic on her face.

"Oh my God, look at you!" she said.

"Quick, pull those clothes off and put a blanket around her," said an unfamiliar man wearing a red cross uniform. "The poor thing might be going into hypothermia."

They scooped me up in a blanket and carried me to Harper's. After plying me with food, hot cocoa, and borrowed clothes from Harper, the man with the red cross, who happened to be Harper's dad, examined me.

"She'll be OK," he said.

"Thank God," my mother said.

Harper's dad left us alone. Mom proceeded to tell me how filled with worry she had been and how I could have died. She also said she understood how upset I was and apologized for not letting me say goodbye to Olympus. Nonetheless, keeping Olympus would not be possible once we left for Mars.

"That's OK," I said.

She furrowed her brow.

"Well, I don't have enough money to pay for her trip after paying for the dolls. Besides, she kept barking, even after I told her not to. So, she won't be allowed on Mars, anyway. And, after the fort, I'm not sure I want to stay here on Earth with her."

"Wait, did you sneak off because you were afraid you couldn't afford her voyage and the dolls?"

"Yes."

My mother buried her face in her hands. "Oh, those lies. All those sweet little lies. They could have killed you."

"I'm not lying, mommy!"

She raised her head and wiped her eyes. "No, you're right, Sweetie. You, did not lie." Suddenly, she hugged me so tightly that breathing became a slight struggle. As grand as my reciprocal hug was, it barely compared.

"Can I talk to Harper, now?" I asked.

"Of course."

She called for Harper, who dragged herself over to the chair across from me, and left the two of us to confront each other without adults in the room. Harper sat with a blank expression and wandering eyes. After a few moments of silence, she shrugged and raised her hands.

"I'm sorry for pushing you on the playground," I said. "I forgive you," she said. She quickly added, "and I really did think we were getting a new dog."

I nodded. "So what are you going to name Olympus?"

"Everest," she said.

My eyes widened and I straightened. "That's what I wanted to name her. Everest is my favorite pup on Paw Patrol."

Harper jumped out of her seat. "Mine too. She's the coolest!"

"She's awesome." We both smiled widely.

"So why didn't you name her Everest?" Harper asked.

"Because my mommy said why name her after the tallest mountain on Earth when we could name her after the tallest mountain in the solar system. So, we named her after a mountain on Mars."

"Oh. What a perfect name. Maybe I'll keep it."

"Thanks," I said with a slight smile. "Can you also point out the red star to her every night, like I do. That's where I'll be living."

"Sure, I'll do that."

"Thanks."

We talked some more about our favorite shows and heroes, sometimes laughing about the funniest episodes. Soon, my mother returned.

"Riley, it's time to go," she said. "Are you ready to say goodbye to Olympus?"

"I am."

"There's No Barking on Mars" is **Russell Weisfield**'s *first published story. He is a Project Manager and Software Developer who lives in Golden, Colorado with his wife, Airedale terrier and young son. When they hike in the mountains, his son never tries to bring the dog along and probably wouldn't try if they moved to Mars.*

Endless, Nameless

Meg Sipos

It starts with strange dreams. Familiar, intimate moments that never happened. Friends she's never met. People she's never actually heard of even though, in her dreams, she could recite their favorite foods and colors, embarrassing stories from their youth, and how they spent their weekends.

In the first dream, Lita's in a house she knows, seated on the leather couch she once spilled an entire glass of red wine on. The mark had left one decent-sized spot of the couch dark and splotchy and had never faded.

In the dream, she's sipping bourbon and staring down at a half-finished puzzle on the coffee table. She's been up all night working on the puzzle, the dim light of morning just beginning to shine through the closed curtains behind her, and she's annoyed at her lack of progress. There's

nothing particularly surprising about the dream. In fact, it's surprisingly mundane compared to the nightmares she's had in the past, compared to fantastical quests and apocalyptic chaos. Except for the fact that it feels so *familiar*. So *real*. And that, in and of itself, is what's so strange about it.

When she wakes from the first dream, a whining siren pierces at her ears, drowning out all other noises. She can't hear the rustling of fabric underneath her, can't hear her husband's snores beside her, even though she knows without a doubt that he *is* snoring. She can't even hear the steady, insistent beeping of the flashing alarm clock on her nightstand.

It takes three hours and a shower before that whining siren becomes a muffled buzz and she's able to hear the world again. It takes another three hours before she realizes she never lived in that house in her dream, never spilled wine on that couch that she never had, and absolutely *hates* puzzles. At least, she *thinks* she hates puzzles.

She's never actually tried her hand at any.

The next time she dreams, Lita dreams of the time she broke her arm. How she tripped and fell over a tennis ball on the court while running suicides with a friend to warm up. How she still tried to play a few sets afterward, despite the growing nausea, despite her fingers feeling loose in their grip while trying desperately to clutch at the racket.

It wasn't until the racket clattered to the ground after a failed attempt at a serve that she had to finally admit something was wrong. How she finally called her husband to pick her up and drive her to the hospital. How he almost didn't believe her, how he thought she might be faking it to get out of socializing.

She wakes from that dream clutching at a throbbing right elbow, her head foggy with agonizing phantom pain.

The thing is, she's never *broken* her arm.

And while she has always considered herself an introvert, she's never even thought of faking an injury to avoid seeing a friend and her husband's *certainly* never accused her of doing such a thing.

As vivid as these dreams are, the things happening in them--the mundane, *real-feeling* things--aren't accurate. That's not her life. *Isn't* her life.

A voice--*her* voice--distorted and distant--tells her to remember anyway.

Remember how it feels, it seems to say.

And in her dreams, she *does* remember.

She remembers how it feels to dive into the ocean and gaze out at a misty landscape of sand and karp and fish, salt stinging her eyes, even though she's never been to the ocean, before she wakes up choking on her own spit and gasping for

breath, her husband tearing himself out of sleep, wide-eyed and helpless, and moving to gently rub her back.

She remembers how it feels to sit in half-seat on an English saddle and soar over fences with a Thoroughbred that liked to play games of tag with her in the fields when they weren't powering through a riding lesson even though she's never set foot in a barn, never seen a horse in person, let alone touch one, let alone *ride one.*

She remembers the wind cutting against her face anyway. The smell of hay. Trying to methodically wipe away the dirt caked on a horse's coat with a curry comb, scraping the mud from the bottom of hooves with a hoof pick, the hair underneath her helmet a mat of sweat.

Then she wakes, numb and confused, with *real* sweat-drenched hair and trembling, achy fingers, skin burning.

That's not her life, she has to remind herself. *Isn't* her life.

Never *was* her life.

And that--that *voice* keeps telling her to remember.

She's content to try to ignore these dreams. To pretend she's not losing her mind, living in some haze of pained confusion, disoriented and unnerved every waking hour. But she supposes she's never been very good at pretending, and she becomes so consumed with all these thoughts--all these memories that can't be memories that she doesn't want to remember--that she more often than not forgets to do her half of the house chores, misses happy hours with friends, and becomes much too distracted for any kind of sex life with her husband.

Her husband, in response, schedules her a doctor's appointment that she can't bring herself to refuse even though people don't really *go* to doctors nowadays. Unless it's a matter of great importance. Or a broken bone.

That's how Lita finds herself perched at the edge of an exam table, staring at the lone picture on the wall that spells out how to properly wash your hands.

The doctor doesn't seem at all surprised or disturbed when she explains her symptoms. Simply nods as she talks about the dreams and the disorientation and the physical pains that seem to manifest while she's sleeping and that rip her awake in the mornings.

After she's done, the doctor jots something down on his notepad as she continues to stare at the poster.

"Lita. Listen very carefully, okay? Your body's shutting down," the doctor tells her after a moment of anxious silence, his voice calm and steady.

Whatever she expected--not that she knew what to expect--it certainly wasn't *that*. Lita tears her gaze away from the instructional poster to study the doctor's face.

He's a young man, with smooth, unwrinkled skin, dark eyes, and rich, feather-like auburn hair. She wonders how long he's been a doctor. How long he went to school to *become* a doctor. When he even started. Maybe he's too young to know what he's talking about, but who is she to say? *She's* not a doctor.

Still...What does that even *mean*? "Am I...dying?"

Dying. The word feels sour on her tongue. Strange and unwelcome.

The doctor offers a blunt "yes."

"But…" that wasn't really possible, was it?

"*How*?" She asks as she squints down at him. "Why?"

Those seem like the only two questions worth asking. Because it doesn't make any sense. Malignant dreams foreshadowing *actual* death. And yet, the doctor looks so certain. So solemn. Like he's seen this before. Like he *knows*.

Lita goes back to staring at the poster as she thinks of the strange, visceral dreams. Of those other lives. Of how short *this one* suddenly feels compared to all those other possibilities.

Maybe those aren't the only two questions worth asking, after all.

So she amends her words to "how long?"

"A month. At most."

A month. That's nothing. That's a...a *blink*. A blip.

Lita tries to breathe, well aware of the unshed tears now blurring her vision.

She feels a soft flutter against her hand and realizes with a spark of surprise that the doctor's pressed a tissue into it. "You do have an option."

And that's the worst part about it all, isn't it? She knows. She *knows* she does.

It's a truth she's never really wanted to think about. *That* option. But it's still constant and lurking and *there*.

The same option that *everyone* has when something terrible and irreversible and potentially fatal happens.

And while she's never actually met anyone who's post-Procedure before, she doesn't know of a single story in which a person was faced with The Procedure and chose not to go through with it. And as soon as the doctor hints at it, she also knows more than she's known anything that it's the only way she'll get to keep living.

"If you want my professional opinion about it, you should consider The Procedure. We will, of course, assist with Relocation afterward. Here," he shuffles through the drawer beside the sink, pulls out a thick green pamphlet, and hands it to her. "This will tell you everything you need to know. And I'm happy to answer any other questions you might have about it. Should I schedule a date?"

Lita tilts her head and stares at the block letters against the green backdrop on the front page, considering, but the tears blur the words together and she just can't bring herself to say yes. Not yet. So she shakes her head, still not trusting herself to speak.

In response to her silence, the doctor nods in understanding.

"Take the pamphlet with you," he urges. "Read it. Talk to your husband. Whatever family or close friends you have. Just...consider it. It's not something you have to decide now. You *do* have some time. Not a lot. But some. Though you'll have to let me know your decision soon so I can schedule what I need to and so that we can discuss Relocation steps. Call me in a week to follow-up, okay? If you don't, I'll reach out myself in two."

Two weeks to decide about The Procedure. About *Relocation*.

Two weeks to decide the rest of her life.

And so Lita walks home, stunned and unsure, torn between wanting to live and not wanting to die.

During dinner, when her husband Mort asks her about the appointment, she settles on honesty. "Doc says the only answer is The Procedure."

The quiet that follows feels unnerving and stuffy and inescapable. Forks scrape against clay plates like a vulture's claw gliding against the glass of the kitchen window.

Mort sets his fork down and leans against the back of his chair. He gazes at Lita for a long moment, green eyes almost glowing under the light of the chandelier above the dining room table. "You should do it."

He sounds as certain as the doctor did.

Lita lets her own fork clatter against her plate as she leans forward. "What? No, of

course not. Have you ever *read* one of those pamphlets? I can't do that to you. To *us*."

"Honey, if it's what you need to stay *alive*"--

"Bull. The Procedure is..." she thinks of the family and friends she's lost to The Procedure. Her parents. Her brother. Mort's sisters. Her best friend. The only coworker-turned-friend she could stand until Jen came along. The list goes on.

They're not dead, of course, but with the necessity of Relocation--of cutting ties--their absence feels just about the same. It's still death. In a way.

"You *know* that you have to endure it too if we want to stay together and that's just...it's bullshit, okay? I'm not doing that to you."

He sighs. "I'm *offering*. We're partners, aren't we? If you need The Procedure so you can live--if you need *us* to get The Procedure so you can live and we can stay together... If that's the only way I don't lose you, then that's what I *want* us to do."

Lita grabs her beer and takes a long gulp. "But I *don't* want you to have..." Again, she thinks of the friends and family they once had, still alive but forever lost to them now. "We know what it does to people, don't we? They find out they're dying...and...they just... The *point* is that the people who go through that whole ordeal, *whatever* it is, leave. They get *Relocated*. And I know that they *have* to. That those are the *conditions* or whatever, but it's like... It's like their pre-Procedure life meant absolutely nothing. And we just get left behind. And I don't want to do that. I don't want to leave people behind. I don't want to leave my life behind...just like..."

"Honey."

She hears the exasperation in Mort's voice and tries to wave off his words with a flip of her hand as she presses on. "In *that* way, they might as well be dead to us anyway, because we don't know who they *are* anymore. They're just gone. They barely even *exist* to us. And I don't *want* that okay? I don't want that for *either* of us. I like my life *here*. I like being *me*."

"You'll still be *you*, sweetheart." Mort says, glowing green eyes softening.

Will I, she wonders. Out loud, she just says, "But it won't be our life. *This* life. It'll be...different."

The word lands flat and hollow and she knows from the slight spark in her husband's face that he doesn't understand the weight of it all.

His soft, assured smile stings. Lita can feel her face flush in discomfort at the sight. He tilts his head a little and nods. Looks at her like this is all natural. Like it's *normal*. "Different, sure. But that doesn't mean bad, does it? That's the thing, honey. You're not giving up your life--our life. We're *saving* it. And we'll still be together. Getting a new *start* to boot. That seems like a pretty good deal to me, don't you think?"

His calm reaction and lack of upset bewilders her.

Mort just got promoted.

He's been talking obsessively about renovating their half-finished basement. About knocking out the one wall and building a home bar to entertain their friends.

Lita can't quite comprehend how he could leave that all behind so willingly.

She stands up in protest. At this point, it's the only thing she can think to do. To leave in a huff of anger and hope that Mort will somehow start to understand where she's coming from even though she doesn't quite understand it herself.

"You don't get it. It's not..." Her words get lost in her throat because she can't articulate *exactly* what it is that she wants to say. Can't quite settle on *exactly* how she feels about all of it. So she just snatches her beer from the table and starts to make her way toward the living room.

Mort calls to her, voice gentle and curious but also tinged with a rigid certainty that's fueling the growing fury inside and making her increasingly uncomfortable.

Everyone around her just seems so *goddamn* certain.

Lita pauses in the archway, back still turned away from him, listening.

"Lita. Like I just said: it's a good deal. I don't understand why you're so reluctant. Plenty of people have gone through with it and we know there's minimal risk. It's standard. And honestly, it's either this and we continue living and we stay happy or...I lose you. You *die*. And that's...I can't even comprehend that, okay? Death is just..." she can hear him taking a swig of his own beer. "It's always seemed so unreal. And I for one would like it to stay that way. I don't want it touching me--touching *us*. You can understand that, can't you? That's why The Procedure is such a wonderful gift. It's allowed our loved ones--and now *us*--the opportunity to keep *living*. Why would you even want to entertain the idea of just *giving up*?"

She stands there, silently, gripping the glass bottle in her hand so tightly that it's a wonder it doesn't shatter from the pressure.

Clearly Mort doesn't understand and she wonders, for the first time it seems, if they even really *know* each other. All these years together, and he can't even acknowledge all the concerning realities about The Procedure? The required Relocation? The invasive operation? Possibly even a lost sense of self, because how could that *not* be a risk when you're forced to leave almost all the pieces of your life behind for the sake of staying alive?

Mort can't react with anything other than pure willingness and certainty even though this impacts every part of *his* life too? Even though he'll lose his current job and his friends? His promotion? His dream entertainment space?

It's distressing to know that Mort can't even *try* to see where she's coming from after ten solid years of marriage.

Maybe he *doesn't* know her.

Maybe she doesn't know *him.*

She stands there for just a moment longer, still not turning around, before striding out of the room.

They don't speak to each other for a week. It's a tense quiet that has Lita squeezing her nails into the palms of her hands every odd hour. She's acutely aware of how dumb it is to hold such a long grudge when facing certain mortality, but she can't stop herself.

She doesn't bother to follow up with the doctor either.

No one can *make* her get The Procedure.

She's at least sure of *that.* And so she tells herself that it's all fine even though it's starting to feel like the end of everything.

On the eighth morning, when Lita bolts awake gasping for air, trying desperately to blink away the screen of red dots blurring her vision, her husband turns to his side, props his right elbow on his pillow and his head on his right hand, and waits for her chokes to subside before finally breaking their week-long silence, "Will you please consider The Procedure?"

She still doesn't have enough air in her lungs to answer with her voice so she merely shakes her head.

Mort sighs and rolls back over, and Lita spends the next five minutes staring at his sheet-covered back while trying to calm her rapid heartbeat by matching the rhythm of his breathing.

They don't speak for the rest of the day.

On the tenth morning, when she wakes to darkness, blind and confused, head pounding, she hears the shuffling of sheets again, "Will you consider The Procedure *now?*"

Her silence is her only answer.

Even without seeing Mort, she knows that *he* knows it's a stubborn refusal.

Then Lita rolls off the bed and, arms outstretched, stumbles toward the bathroom, where she stands underneath the showerhead until the water turns ice cold and she can see again.

That same day, she meets her friend Jen for a brunch date they scheduled months ago.

They're sitting in a corner booth at the diner down the street from her house and Lita's staring out the window as she twirls a fork around her uneaten scrambled eggs. They've already gone through all the motions of small talk and she's not much of a conversationalist at the moment, with the dreams and The Procedure on her mind, and Jen clearly notices her silence.

After the waiter refills their coffee mugs, Jen stirs two packs of hazelnut creamer into her cup before leaning forward, elbows on the sticky table, fingers clasped around the drink. She asks why Lita's so uncharacteristically quiet.

For a moment, Lita's stunned by the question.

Is she *uncharacteristically* quiet?

She's never thought of herself as a particularly talkative person before.

She stares at the dancing liquid in Jen's mug before meeting her friend's concerned eyes. "Do you ever dream that you're...well you're sort of you, but you're, uh, someone else?"

Jen's eyebrows furrow and her head tilts in confusion. "I have absolutely no idea what you mean."

Lita finally puts her fork down. "Like, you ever have dreams where it's definitely you, right?--At least, you *think* it's definitely you--but your life is all, uh...*different*? I mean, like...another life?

And it's not like it's a particularly *exciting* existence or anything. It's just, like I said, another life. You ever dream of other lives so vividly that it feels like you *have* to have lived them and they make you question what's actually real and what's the lie?"

Jen's fingers unclasp from the steaming mug of coffee and she hunches forward, resting her chin on the palm of her right hand. Her searching brown eyes, glowing amber underneath the fluorescent lights of the diner, make Lita's skin itch. "Hm. Well, that's a new one. Can't say that I have, no."

Jen probably thinks she's crazy now. Still, Lita can't help the pressing *"never?"* that escapes her lips.

Jen shakes her head, eyebrows still scrunched. "Nope. Never. What's with the...I mean, obviously you're on edge. And those dreams sound...confusing, I guess? I mean, you haven't shared any of the juicy details, but... Seriously, what's up? You go to a doctor or anything?"

Lita takes a sip of her own coffee while mulling over her response. "Went the other day, actually. Cause I wake up from the dreams so disoriented and so often in pain and I've just been a mess. So Mort scheduled an appointment." She pauses as she prepares for her next few words. "Turns out I gotta get The Procedure."

Jen lets out a deep sigh and leans against the back of the booth, lips now tipped in a growing frown. "Oh. *Oh.*" She doesn't seem *surprised*, but she does seem...disappointed?

"Yeah." Lita takes another sip of coffee and watches her friend process the information. Admittedly, she feels a flare of happiness at Jen's apparent distress. At the same time, she feels wary of the disappointment visible on her friend's face. The guilt in her gut over delivering such terrible news doesn't help matters.

"That really *sucks*. Like a lot. I'm definitely going to miss you. I hope you know that."

Whatever reaction Lita was expecting from Jen, though, it certainly wasn't this bare acceptance. And so she finds herself admitting, "I'm not sure about going through with it."

Jen blinks. Then her brown eyes, still glowing amber under the lighting, narrow in surprise. "Wait. What? What do you mean?"

Lita shrugs, starting to feel the same kind of discomfort she feels when Mort presses the issue every morning she wakes from one of those terrible dreams-- memories?---*dreams.*

"I just mean that I'm not sure I wanna do it."

Jen's frown deepens and her eyes fog over. A long, unnerving silence follows.

Lita's starting to think she may have broken her friend. But then Jen shakes her head and blinks the fog away.

"You're not sure you want to..." Jen's dazed voice, full of bitter awe, fades into the other chatter around them.

Lita shifts in her seat, skin itching at the unreadable glare Jen's fixed her with. "Well, I mean. Answer me honestly, Jen. After losing family and friends to Relocation, would *you* do it?"

Jen's eyes widen again, but not with confusion. This time, those eyes are twinkling with the same certainty Lita saw in the doctor and in Mort.

Jen looks at Lita like it's the most obvious answer in the world. "Of course I would. That's just how it works. Everybody does it. It's such a wonderful gift."

Lita assesses her friend. Her friend who sounds so incredibly sure. Who sounds like she *knows*. She has to ask. "Wait a second. Have you...did *you*..."

"What? Get The Procedure?"

Lita nods, waiting.

"Nah, not me." Jen says as she takes a bite of her toast. "I mean, my dad did several years ago. And my friend from college. And I'll obviously do it too whenever it inevitably comes to that because that's just how it works. Anything to keep living the life, right?" Lita can hear the veiled accusation in that rhetorical question, can hear Jen's horrified consternation at being confronted with someone who might actually *choose* death over The Procedure. Because that simply didn't happen. "But as of yet? Nope."

Lita met Jen two years ago, but they'd never really talked about what their lives were like before they started working together and became friends. Come to think of it, Lita doesn't even know where the woman's originally from.

Suddenly, she feels compelled to ask.

"What were you doing before, anyway?"

"Before?"

"Before moving here. Before taking a job at the agency. What did you do? Where did you say you were from again? Actually, it's weird, but I don't think I ever asked. And if I ever did, then I apologize, because I don't quite remember the answer."

Jen puts her half-eaten toast back on her plate and pours her fourth packet of creamer into her coffee. "Oh, really? Well, nothing special. Just the same old thing really, but in a different place. Just got transferred, I guess."

"And what place was that?"

"Just some small southern town," Jen says.

But where? Lita wonders. Instead, she asks, "Do you miss it?"

Jen scrunches her eyebrows again, as if the question were difficult to process. "Uh, sure. I mean, probably a little. But I'm not one to dwell on the past, really. I like where I'm at now. I like it here."

Lita nods, finally taking a bite of her scrambled eggs. "Of course. Yeah. I get that. But, like, what was your favorite thing about where you lived before?"

Again, she can feel it. Something's not right. Something's *wrong*.

And Lita knows, with increasing dread, that it has something to do with The Procedure. The Procedure that everyone says is *normal*. Common.

Expected.

"It was a pretty boring, sleepy town, Lita. If I'm being honest, I don't remember much about it. What I can tell you is that I like it much better here. I like my friends and I like who I am and I'm really going to miss you because you were a big part of all of that."

Lita wants to press more, but the more she thinks about it, the more she knows that she can't really blame Jen for such vague answers.

If anyone asked her what she and Mort had been doing before they moved here she probably would have answered the same way.

There was nothing special about the small northern town they lived in before. Nothing special about her job or his. That part of their life wasn't particularly memorable.

The guilt in her gut swells.

Maybe she really *is* just acting absurd about all of this.

Maybe there's nothing wrong.

Other than her body shutting down and her needing The Procedure, anyway.

And yet, Lita *still* feels this incredible urge to know what Jen's life was like before they knew each other. Something about it just isn't sitting right. She can *feel* it. At least, she *thinks* she can. But she doesn't push.

77

Because, just like Jen, she likes where she's at in life. She likes her husband and her friends and her job and this town. She likes everything about it.

She hates the idea of losing all of that.

On the fourteenth night, as she and Mort finish dinner, Lita finds that she still can't really remember much about the life they led before moving into this house. Even trying to think about it in her waking hours has been giving her a headache.

So she breaks their continued mutual silence to ask, "do you ever think about our old life? The one we had before we moved here? Do you remember what it was like?"

Mort simply shakes his head. "This is our life. And when we finally get The Procedure, after you stop acting so childish about it, then whatever comes next will be our life. Sure, this chapter has been great, but every chapter has to come to an end eventually, doesn't it? That's just the way it works. I do like it here, sweetheart. I don't want you to think that I don't like our life the way it is now. But I also know that I'll like the next adventure just as much. Who knows? Maybe even more."

"You mean you *never* think about before? At all? You're *not* actually wondering about what might possibly come after...*after*?"

In response, Mort lifts himself from the table and walks over to Lita to stand behind her chair. He rests his hands on her shoulders and begins to massage his fingers into her knotted muscles. "What does it matter, honey? The here and now is the only thing that's important."

"But"--

"Now let me ask *my* question. Will you please stop with this nonsense and just schedule The Procedure?"

She realizes, quite suddenly, that it's been two weeks since her doctor's appointment.

The doctor hasn't called to follow-up.

Strange, she thinks, but she pushes that thought aside. "Mort, I just"--

The ready words fade on her tongue as Mort's fingers become firmer--*harsher*. It's impossible to relax into the massage as his hands go from gentle to rough.

He presses his weight into her knots in a painful way, in a way that steals her breath and breeds frantic realization. His hands inch closer to her neck and collarbone.

And then Mort's right arm wraps around her neck while his left hand presses down against her shoulder to keep her still.

Panic and dread and fear flare inside.

Lita knows she should be trying to fight him off, knows that this *isn't right*, but by the time she finally starts to claw at his sleeves with her own trembling hands it's too late.

The firm pressure around her neck increases, robbing more of her breath--*all* of her breath--as she struggles against the tightening grip.

Her red-dotted vision blurs with unshed tears.

Mort shushes her as he continues to squeeze. He tells her it's going to be fine. "I'm sorry, sweetheart, but we just can't wait any longer for you to make the right call. Like your brother used to say: better to ask for forgiveness later."

A familiar darkness claims her and she falls into another vivid dream.

As Lita dreams, she remembers.

Lita remembers packing a car full of games and wine and beer and blankets and flashlights and the fixings for s'mores. Prep for a drive down to the cabin her in-laws offered them for the week for a romantic getaway.

She remembers their car careening off the darkened highway after having been struck by a truck driver who had lost

78

control, veering into oncoming traffic. Into *them.*

She remembers crawling out of a shattered windshield, bloody palms pressing into glass shards as she stumbled over to Mort's mangled body.

He was slumped against the trunk of a tree, his legs bent at odd angles, his hand twisted, his head lolling listlessly to his chest.

Lita remembers the sirens and Mort's desperate wheezing as he sputtered out specks of blood that painted his lips and chin red.

She remembers her own breathless agony as she dragged her damaged body toward him, her quivering hand clutching at his limp fingers, and the numb shock that settled in as she took in his injuries.

She begged him not to leave her.

"I hear sirens." Her voice was shaky and desperate. "Just hold on, okay? I hear sirens. An ambulance will come, I know it, and they'll take us in for an emergency Procedure. It's going to be okay."

He didn't seem to understand her promise.

She looked down at his twisted limbs and lifted a hand to his face. Brushed her fingertips against his cheek.

"We're going to live."

Maybe if she believed it enough, that would make it true. Make it certain.

"Just hold on a little longer. This is what The Procedure is for, you know. We still have a life to live together."

"A life," he repeated, blue eyes unseeing for a moment before they finally focused on Lita. Then his body twitched and his not-twisted hand limply grabbed at Lita's ripped shirt.

When she glanced down, she was surprised to find a growing stain. Her own blood.

The pain of the injury was noticeably absent, consumed by panic and desperation and a growing numbness.

She understood, quite clearly, that they were dying. That help might not come in time.

But that couldn't be right, could it? Because that's what The Procedure was *for.* To help. To give life. Another chance. *More time.*

Dying was such a strange, horrible thing. She never thought she would have to feel what it was like. Never thought it would touch them.

"Please, Lita." Mort wheezed. "Even if they don't make it in time to help me...*please*...you'll still do it, right? I don't want to die, but I can feel it, Lita. I can *feel* it. Please don't. Please don't die, Lita."

Just as quickly as his frantic burst of begging started, it stopped. The life in his eyes sparked and then faded. Lita knew, as she watched, that it was too late for Mort.

And she remembers the drive in the ambulance and the doctor and his promise to make it right again. Well, not *completely* right. They couldn't operate on someone who'd been dead for at least an hour by the time they got to the closest hospital. But she remembers the doctor promising, all the same, to help her with her grief--to erase it.

It's a service we provide.

She remembers the doctor asking her to tell him about Mort. And she did. She told the doctor about Mort's favorite foods and the kind of music he liked. She told the doctor about Mort's obsession with pilsners and about the cities he wanted to visit and about his ridiculous humor and how much he enjoyed cooking strange dishes and making her try his weird culinary creations. How he liked to stand outside in a storm and let the rain soak into his skin. The little marshmallows he still insisted on putting in his hot cocoa. The way he checked behind the shower curtain any time he entered the bathroom in the same way a child might check under the bed or in the back of the closet for monsters. She told the doctor everything.

And after, she got The Procedure, just as she had so many times before that, except *this* time, she went through it alone.

She didn't want to live without Mort. But she didn't want to die either.

And he had begged her not to.

When she woke, though, Mort was standing above her hospital bed, staring down at her with a fond smile and bright green eyes.

In her Post-Procedure haze, she muttered something about them glowing.

As she continues to dream, Lita remembers that Mort's eyes--the *real* Mort's eyes--were a deep, murky blue.

Most of all, Lita remembers her decision to *live*. Because it was what Mort wanted.

She also remembers wondering--briefly, before her operation, before the doctor promised her that she wouldn't have to carry the pain of that loss--how Mort could be so cruel as to demand such a thing from her.

Lita remembers all of The Procedures she's had since losing Mort. And she remembers all the times she's woken up to his glowing green eyes.

When Lita comes to, she's lying on a gurney in a sterile hospital room, the young doctor--the same one who's been with her since that horrible car accident--looking down on her with a soft, knowing expression.

Lita's a little surprised to find herself not strapped to the table. But it's apparent from the doctor's face that he doesn't believe she'll choose to run out the door.

Not that she thinks she could if she wanted to, her limbs too heavy and stone-like.

She can also tell that *he* can tell that she's starting to remember everything.

"Haven't heard from you in two weeks." The doctor says. "Mort's programmed to step in if needed. That's how you wanted it. And, well. This is me. Following up. Mort's already gone in for re-programming. So. Are you ready for The Procedure now?"

She still can't quite process the reality before her.

She thinks about her dreams. Her *memories*.

She thinks about all the times she's come in before.

She couldn't possibly have lived all those lives in *this* body, but...she clutches at her head, a wave of pain her reward for trying to understand her situation.

"I'm a...copy?" The words stumbling from her mouth feel foreign. Unreal.

But the core of her knows that the word is also *right*.

The same mind. The same consciousness, at least. But different bodies.

So many bodies.

So many bodies that felt like hers but *not* at the same time. That fit but *didn't*.

She remembers that the doctor *did* kill the person she used to be. *All* the people she used to be. She can recall, so vividly, what it feels like to teeter on the edge of death. That hopeless feeling that spreads into her bones before she's pulled back from the abyss.

Even if she knows what's real now, she'd be lying if she said any of it made sense. But she supposes that, at least in her *lives*, nothing ever does.

It would be strange for things to start making sense now.

The doctor leans against the wall and crosses his arms. "A copy of a copy, even. If you wanted to get technical about it. You usually do."

"I do?"

As soon as he says it, she knows it's true.

His smirk fades and he offers a sad smile. "We've been here before."

"I...I don't remember. Why don't I remember?"

"It doesn't suit the programming."

Like it's as simple as that.

Remember, that voice in her head urges.

And so she closes her eyes and lets more of her dreams--her *memories* wash over her until she finds the one she's looking for.

Her last Procedure.

She looks back at the doctor. "I...I remember now. Why do I remember *now*?"

It doesn't make sense for her to remember their last conversation so vividly without the dreams and her body malfunctioning and the horrid feeling of going crazy.

"Consent is important. The Procedure can't happen without consent."

"But I'll forget. All of this. After."

"Yes."

"Why?"

The doctor leans forward, eyes wide, voice insistent. "Because you have to *believe* in yourself. You can't question your reality. You can't question whether or not"--

"I'm real. This life is real. *Anything* is real."

The doctor nods, his sad smile softening. "Yes."

"And if I do anyway? Question it, I mean. What then?"

"You know what happens, Lita. We've been through this so many times before. The body shuts down. The consciousness rejects it."

That's what's been happening, she realizes. She's been *remembering*.

Except it doesn't suit the programming. It doesn't suit this...*body*.

Her being is incompatible with her...*vessel*.

How strange to finally have an answer.

How strange that it's finally starting to make sense.

The doctor moves toward the window. Closing the blinds, he tells her, "You don't have to go through with it, you know. You can cease to exist whenever you please."

"I can...what?"

"Cease to exist. Others have. By choice, I mean. And others, well, others weren't lucky enough to have a say. But just a few."

Lita thinks about Mort's mangled body and his thinning breath and the desperation in his weakened voice as he begged her not to die even if he didn't make it into the operation room in time. "Mort?" she whispers, even though she already knows.

"Mort."

Mort's not Mort. Simply a physical manifestation of her own memories. But not *Mort*.

She thinks about all the things she told the doctor about Mort, big and small. Simple and complicated. *It's a service we provide.*

She thinks about the glowing green eyes--so different from those deep, murky blue orbs.

"*Why*?" She asks, tears in her eyes.

"Why *wouldn't* we offer to eradicate the grief if we could? Get rid of the loss? We did it with your consent, Lita, I can promise you that. You agreed after we explained that attachments make for an easier operation and an easier transition."

"But..my...my *husband*..."

Her husband's dead. *Truly* dead.

The loss she feels at the knowledge threatens to drown her.

"I realize it's a difficult thing to process. But it won't mean a thing post-Procedure. And we did a decent job replicating him based on your notes, didn't we? I thought so. I mean, you've never noticed before. But please. Take a moment if you have to. I understand it's a lot to absorb." He pauses. "If you'd rather choose CTE in lieu of The Procedure, we would just need you to write a will specifying what you would like us to do with your assets, including whether you'd like us to retire Mort."

"I..." Lita thinks of her dreams. All those other lives. *Her* lives. Lives she's lived that she only now remembers. Lives she could *still* live.

She wonders what's better--living without the memories or dying with the knowledge and the pain of every breath-filled moment.

But it's what Mort *wanted*. It's what he begged from her with his own dying breaths.

And she'll keep her promise.

And this time, she'll find a way to remember without triggering her mind's rejection of her new body. She'll find a way to remember without deteriorating. Without *dying*.

She'll remember *her* Mort. She'll remember who she *is*. She'll remember everything.

She'll find a way to do it. She *will*.

Then she won't have to wonder why it's all so important because she'll already know.

She'll be *herself*.

She won't have to question or dread the gift The Procedure offers if she can find a safe way to remember.

Lita meets the doctor's waiting gaze. "I'm ready for The Procedure."

As Lita transitions into the waking world, her own voice, both familiar and strange, lingers in her head like a dull, persistent echo, urging her to remember.

Meg Sipos *holds a BFA and MFA in creative writing. Her work has appeared or is forthcoming in MoonPark Review, Lammergeier Magazine, The Ghost Story, Bath Flash Fiction Volume Four: With One Eye on the Cows, Quantum Shorts, Liminality: A Magazine of Speculative Poetry, Welter, Dark Hearts: Tales of Twisted Love, 21st Century Ghost Stories Vol. II, and Futures. She recently co-founded* The Other Folk, *a blog about the many faces of horror in film, art, music, and literature.*

Film, TV and Books

Reviews by Mark Bilsborough and Sandra Baker

MCU round-up:

Spider Man: Far from Home
Shang-Chi: Legend of the Ten Rings
The Eternals
Hawkeye

There's been plenty going on in Marvel-land since we last covered Stan Lee's astoundingly rich legacy as it rumbles into Phase Four of its Marvel Cinematic Universe, now spreading its tendrils into TV thanks to Disney+

The MCU has delivered more hits than misses over the years, but some of its projects have been more indifferent than others (What-If, for instance), and *Eternals* arguably falls into that category. Based on Jack Kirby's comic creations, the superpowered Eternals are sent to Earth by the Celestials to eradicate the Deviants. The conflict has been going on for centuries, but things really flare up – and humanity's in the way.

Unlike most recent Marvel offerings, this is a film of (mostly) entirely new characters, and that arguably robs it of its foundations. It's similar to the ill-fated TV series *the Inhumans*, and some say Marvel only developed either to have a wholly owned alternative to the hugely-popular *X-Men*, for which, frustratingly, they didn't hold the broadcast rights. But now Disney have bought Paramount and have the rights back, why would we need the Eternals?

Another film with mostly new (to film) characters, *Shang-Chi and the Legend of the Ten Rings*, fares rather better. Apart from the uncomfortable revelation that I've been mispronouncing 'Shang-Chi' for years, this film delivers the expected Marvel experience: outsider heroes, conflicted villains, plenty of action more than a hint of the supernatural. It has another go at introducing The Mandarin as the main villain. This time he's Shang-Chi's father, but there's also a nod to the Iron Man version – Ben Kingsley's comic turn as the actor Trevor Slattery. For me, though, neither of these iterations of the iconic Marvel villain really work, but I've got some sympathy for the studio – the Mandarin was modelled on Fu Manchu and that's surely not a caricature that translates into today's global (and hopefully more enlightened) marketplace. This film mostly works, though, and it's good to see Shang-Chi finally emerge into the MCU.

Then there's *Spider-Man, Far From Home*. Well, was it worth all the hype? There's no way to review this film without spoilers, unfortunately, so you'll have to see for yourselves. I will say, though, that this is an impressive addition to the series and the first post pandemic Marvel movie that really feels like a Marvel movie, with a packed cast and some truly bad bad guys. With Iron Man no longer around Doctor Strange is the crossover character and he's in a lot of this film – but then, lots of characters are in this film a lot. Happy bits, sad bits and exciting bits – definitely must-watch if you enjoyed any of the other films (and definitely one to leave 'til last if you haven't, because you'll have about as much clue as the bored seven year old sitting next to me in the cinema if you don't).

But Marvel have been busy in lockdown, so we've also got the small screen *Hawkeye* limited series to work through. Here, Clint Barton's effectively retired from active Avengers duty, but his past (as the maverick Ronin) is beginning to catch up with him. He preps up a replacement Hawkeye (Kate Bishop) who, surely, will gravitate to the Avengers proper in time. The plot is twisty-complex and the action loud and predictably over the top, and then there's the Kingpin, making a very welcome return from the ill-fated Netflix/Marvel partnership shows (and maybe he's not the only one, if you believe the *Spider Man* rumours). *Hawkeye* is very watchable – pity it's taken Marvel so long to let him spread his wings.

The Amber Crown
Jacey Bedford

The Amber Crown is Jacey Bedford's seventh book for DAW, the legendary US-based fantasy and science fiction publisher. She's already gained much commercial and critical success with 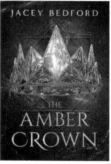 her *Psi-Tech* science fiction trilogy and her *Rowankind* fantasies, and now she's back with another magic and mayhem romp with The Amber Crown, set in a fictional (and fantastical) Eastern Europe sometime in the Middle Ages,

We've got war and palace intrigue in *The Amber Crown*. In Zavonia, the King is dead, the man suspected of ordering him killed is on the throne and the Queen is on the run. The assassin – Lind – isn't your usual ice-cool killer and when his mysterious employers give him a very unwelcome new commission, his principles become very stretched.

Most of the King's guards are dead, killed by the new regime. But their Captain, Valdas, survives and is accused of the murder, but is desperate to avenge his

King and his fallen Guard friends. And then there's the 'landstrider' healer, Mirza, who has more than a hint of magic about her to accompany her increasingly disfiguring facial birthmark, treated with suspicion by her people who are, nonetheless, dependent on her talents.

These three characters are very different but they share a common thread: they're all shunned, for one reason of another, and they're all determined to restore stability to what rapidly becomes a fractious political (and military) environment. With Zavonia about to slip into devastation and conflict due to the neglect, incompetence and capriciousness of the new King, can the three unlikely allies find out who's really responsible for the darkness destroying the Kingdom and save the day?

In many ways this is classic fantasy, soundly based in vaguely recognisable almost-real parts of middle Europe in the time of flintlocks and fighting, as kings and nobles position for power. So much so Game of Thrones, but The Amber Crown is its own beast – engaging, high paced and full of fascinating characters. I didn't say likeable because some of them certainly aren't – but the dubious ones have just that hint of redemptive promise to keep you reading.

The storyline moves quickly in this novel and it's not bogged down with too much in the way of extraneous worldbuilding – like all good books, hints are enough to build a vivid picture and we can do the rest. This world and these characters are set up nicely for future stories, but this narrative arc has a proper ending – we're not going to feel cheated by unanswered questions. *The Amber Crown* is a well-constructed character driven page-turner and a great introduction to Jacey Bedford's writing.

The Every
Dave Eggers

The follow-up to 'The Circle', this book did not disappoint. Speculative fiction at its best – so close to a potential reality that it's disturbing. Is Alexa listening in on our  every conversation? Are we so afraid of saying or doing the wrong thing that we are afraid to say or do anything at all? At times hilarious and quite often terrifying, the novel follows the attempts of the attempts of an individual - our protagonist 'Delaney' -to bring down the huge global corporation – The Every – that dominates and monopolises all aspects of day-to-day life.

The problem Delaney faces is that The Every is beloved by everyone. Life is easier, more convenient, less threatening. Those that object to having their lives micro-managed by this global giant are known as 'Trogs' and have nothing but the pity of those who have embraced the technology of The Every.

Delaney's plan – after she has begun working for The Every – is to invent increasingly ridiculous apps, designed to show people how they are being manipulated. However, her ideas are embraced rather than rejected. Her first idea – an app called AuthentiFriend which enables you to see if your friends are lying to you or not – becomes massively popular and frustratingly, no-one seems to see or even consider how damaging it is.

The book explores - with excruciating perception – how society is in danger of surrendering control and freewill to the giants of the internet. How much will people sacrifice for convenience? In some ways this book is as impactful as '1984' and yet it could be seen just as a gentle poke at the tech giants that are now so embroiled in our lives.

Dave Eggers has a straightforward, compelling writing style that allows the reader to develop their response to his message in their own time. It's not a preachy book, but it will make you think about switching off Alexa and cookies and location services and shopping suggestions and …

Screams from the Void
Anne Tibbets

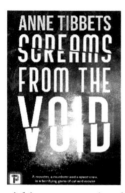

This one's a bit of a roller coaster. Scary sci-fi in the vein of Alien and Escape Velocity, it moves at pace and lurches from twist to turn with satisfying inevitability. The *Demeter* is a freighter out in deep space, picking up exotic plants from around the thinly explored fringes of human expansion. It turns out, though, that they've picked up something dangerously unexpected.

You know the drill: a small crew, packed with a mixture of incompetents and malcontents, picked off one by one by a force they can't control. Ensign Reina is our point of view character, an engineer who almost single-handedly keeps the ship going while her useless boss Osric yells and harangues her. She's also got to deal with her abusive ex-boyfriend, Morven, who shifts from full on amorous to outright hostile in his efforts to win her over (or drag her back) into their relationship.

The *Demeter* is only a couple of weeks away from Earth when the Bridge crew comes across something unexpected in the air vents, a 'foreign biological' they picked up earlier in the trip. Needless to say, the 'biological' has claws. It's also got a superstrong hide and a chameleon-like ability to hide in plain sight. And it's hungry.

There's blood, there's gore, and, with every officer apart from the ship's cook either dead or missing, before long the plucky Reina and her dwindling band of fellow ensigns are fighting for their lives.

Working out who the real monster here is central to this book and drives the narrative. It's not covering any new ground, and the way the plot plays out is predictable, but it's edge of the seat nonetheless, a competent and enjoyable descent into terror. As someone once said, in space, no-one can hear you scream.

Wyldblood Magazine #7, Winter 2022.
© 2022 Wyldblood Press and contributors.

Publisher: Wyldblood Press, Thicket View, Bakers Lane, Maidenhead SL6 6PX UK. www.wyldblood.com **Editor:** Mark Bilsborough. **Fiction editor** Sandra Baker. **First readers:** Vaughan Stanger, Mike Lewis, Rebecca Ruvinsky, Bailey Spencer. **Subscriptions:** 4 issues epub/mobi/pdf delivered to your inbox £11. 4 issue print subscriptions £22. www.wyldblood.com/magazine Single issues available worldwide via Amazon and from Wyldblood:

Submissions: we are regularly open for submissions of flash fiction, short stories and novels – check our website for our current status and requirements. We are a paying market. We also need artwork, people to review us, and people to review *for* us. Email contact@wyldblood.com

ISBN 978-1-914417-05-4

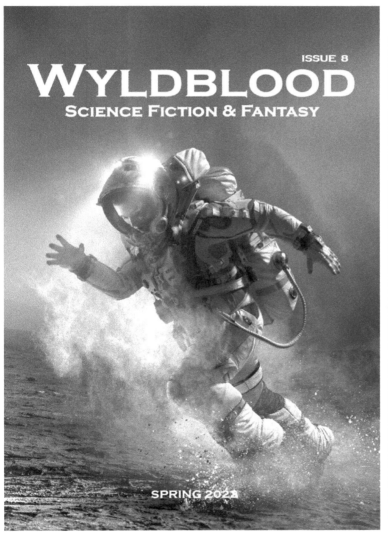

CPSIA information can be obtained
at www.ICGtesting.com
Printed in the USA
LVHW021322180122
708754LV00006B/534